LATIN'S NOT SO TOUGH!

LEVEL FOUR

A Classical Latin Worktext
by
Karen Mohs

Dear Parent/Teacher:

Welcome to the Latin Workbook Level Four!

In this workbook, students review the Latin alphabet, vocabulary, and grammar introduced in Levels One through Three. They learn the remaining declensions and conjugations (present active indicative only), various macron and accenting rules, as well as additional vocabulary. Sentences are contrived and simplified to afford practice with the forms the student has learned.

Remove the flashcard pages at the end of the workbook, cut out the words, and copy, paste, or tape them onto 3 by 5 inch cards.

Begin use of flashcards on page 7 of the workbook. Your student should put a check mark in the box at the bottom of each page when daily flashcard work is completed. Please refer to "Flashcard Tips" in the appendix.

Please take a moment to look through the appendix pages. There you will find a glossary, an index, and other helpful resources such as paradigms for the conjugations and declensions taught in this workbook. An answer key is available, as well as quizzes/exams, flashcards on a ring, and an audio pronunciation CD or cassette tape.

References for this series include *First Year Latin* by Charles Jenney, Jr., *Second Year Latin* by Charles Jenney, Jr., and *The New College Latin & English Dictionary* by John C. Traupman, Ph.D.

Keep having fun!

Copyright © 2000 by Karen Mohs
All rights reserved. No part of this publication may be reproduced without prior permission of the author.

ISBN-13: 978-1-931842-65-5
ISBN-10: 1-931842-65-5

Greek 'n' Stuff
P.O. Box 882
Moline, IL 61266-0882
www.greeknstuff.com

Revised 10/04

This workbook
belongs to me:

_____

(student's name)

because
I'M LEARNING LATIN
Level Four!

TABLE OF CONTENTS

Lesson 1 1-6
Pronunciation review

Lesson 2 7-11
Vocabulary review - Part 1

Lesson 3 12-16
Vocabulary review - Part 2

Lesson 4 17-21
Vocabulary review - Part 3

Lesson 5 22-26
Vocabulary review - Part 4

Lesson 6 27-28
First conjugation present active indicative review

Lesson 7 29-38
First declension, second declension -us and -ius review (all cases)

Lesson 8 39-40
Principal parts of verbs

Lesson 9 41-48
Macrons, syllables, and accents

Lesson 10 49-52
New vocabulary - Part 1

Lesson 11 53-56
New vocabulary - Part 2

Lesson 12 57-60
New vocabulary - Part 3

Lesson 13 61-66
New vocabulary - Part 4

Lesson 14 67-68
Sum - the "being" verb

Lesson 15 69-70
Ablative of accompaniment

Lesson 16 71-74
"Declension" - second declension neuter, second declension -er

Lesson 17 75-78
Third declension

Latin Workbook - Level 4
Copyright © 2000 by Karen Mohs

Lesson 18 79-82
Third declension i-stem

Lesson 19 83-86
"Conjugation" - second conjugation

Lesson 20 87-90
Third conjugation

Lesson 21 91-94
New vocabulary - Part 5

Lesson 22 95-98
New vocabulary - Part 6

Lesson 23 99-102
New vocabulary - Part 7

Lesson 24 103-108
New vocabulary - Part 8

Lesson 25 109-112
Third declension neuter

Lesson 26 113-118
Questions

Lesson 27 119-122
Third conjugation i-stem

Lesson 28 123-126
Fourth declension

Lesson 29 127-130
Fourth conjugation

Lesson 30 131-138
Fifth declension

Lesson 31 139-142
New vocabulary - Part 9

Lesson 32 143-146
New vocabulary - Part 10

Lesson 33 147-154
New vocabulary - Part 11

Lesson 34 155-160
Sentence practice

Lesson 35 161-165
Final review - Part 1

Lesson 36 166-170
Final review - Part 2

Latin Workbook - Level 4
Copyright © 2000 by Karen Mohs

Appendix

Latin - English Glossary 171-173

English - Latin Glossary 175-177

Latin Alphabet 179

Special Sounds 179

Macrons, Syllables, and Accents 180

Principal Parts of the Latin Verb 181

Word Order 181

Moods of the Latin Verb 181

Voices of the Latin Verb 182

Gender and Case of the Latin Noun 182

Special Case Uses 182

First Conjugation 183

Second Conjugation 183

Third Conjugation 184

Third I-Stem Conjugation 184

Fourth Conjugation 185

The "Being" Verb - Present Indicative 185

First Declension 186

Second Declension 186

Second Declension -ius 187

Second Declension -er (as in puer) 187

Second Declension -er (as in ager) 188

Second Declension Neuter 188

Third Declension (as in frāter) 189

Third Declension (as in soror) 189

Third Declension I-Stem 190

Third Declension Neuter 191

Fourth Declension 191

Fifth Declension (as in diēs) 192

Fifth Declension (as in spēs) 192

Index 193-194

Flashcard Tips 195

Latin Workbook - Level 4
Copyright © 2000 by Karen Mohs

Latin Workbook - Level 4
Copyright © 2000 by Karen Mohs

Lesson 1

LATIN PRONUNCIATION REVIEW

Ā ā

Say "a" as in *father*.

A a

Say "a" as in *idea*.

B b

Say "b" as in *boy*.

C c

Say "c" as in *cat*.

D d

Say "d" as in *dog*.

Ē ē

Say "ey" as in *obey*.

E e

Say "e" as in *bet*.

F f

Say "f" as in *fan*.

G g

Say "g" as in *go*.

H h

Say "h" as in *hat*.

Ī ī

Say "i" as in *machine*.

I i

Say "i" as in *sit*.

Latin Workbook - Level 4
Copyright © 2000 by Karen Mohs

1

LATIN PRONUNCIATION REVIEW

K k
K k
Say "**k**" as in *king*.

P p
P p
Say "**p**" as in *pit*.

L l
L l
Say "**l**" as in *land*.

Q q
Qu qu
Say "**qu**" as in *quit*.

M m
M m
Say "**m**" as in *man*.

R r
R r
Say "**r**" as in *run*.

N n
N n
Say "**n**" as in *nut*.

S s
S s
Say "**s**" as in *sit*.

Ō ō
Ō ō
Say "**o**" as in *note*.*

T t
T t
Say "**t**" as in *tag*.

O o
O o
Say "**o**" as in *omit*.*

Ū ū
Ū ū
Say "**u**" as in *rule*.

*Although both Latin "o" sounds are "long," the ō as in *note* is held longer than the o as in *omit*.

2

Latin Workbook - Level 4
Copyright © 2000 by Karen Mohs

LATIN PRONUNCIATION REVIEW

U u — U u — Say "**u**" as in *put*.

V v — V v — Say "**w**" as in *way*.

X x — X x — Say "**ks**" as in *socks*.

Ȳ ȳ — Ȳ ȳ — Form lips to say "**oo**," but say "**ee**" instead. (Hold the sound longer than Latin y.)

Y y — Y y — Form lips to say "**oo**," but say "**ee**" instead. (Hold the sound shorter than Latin ȳ.)

Z z — Z z — Say "**dz**" as in *adze*.

ae — ae — Say "*aye*."

au — au — Say "**ow**" as in *now*.

ei — ei — Say "**ei**" as in *neighbor*.

eu — eu — Say "*ay-oo*" as one syllable.

oe — oe — Say "**oy**" as in *joy*.

ui — ui — Say "**uee**" as in *queen*.

Latin Workbook - Level 4
Copyright © 2000 by Karen Mohs

3

LATIN PRONUNCIATION REVIEW

bs — bs
Say "*ps*."

bt — bt
Say "*pt*."

ch — ch
Say "**ch**" as in *character*.

gu — gu
Say "**gu**" as in *anguish*.

i — i
Say "**y**" as in *youth*.

ph — ph
Say "**ph**" as in *phone*.

su — su
Say "**su**" as in *suave*.

th — th
Say "**th**" as in *thick*.

Circle the correct sounds.

ō	"o" in *omit*	"o" in *note*
bt	"*pt*"	"*bt*"
e	"e" in *bet*	"ey" in *obey*

eu	"*ay-oo*"	"**uee**" in *queen*
a	"a" in *father*	"a" in *idea*
ī	"i" in *machine*	"i" in *sit*

4

Latin Workbook - Level 4
Copyright © 2000 by Karen Mohs

LATIN PRONUNCIATION REVIEW

Match the letters to their sounds.

Z z	dz in *adze*	Y y	w in *way*	
B b	g in *go*	Ō ō	form lips to say "oo," say "ee" instead (held shorter)	
G g	d in *dog*	Ȳ ȳ	i in *machine*	
Q q	b in *boy*	I i	form lips to say "oo," say "ee" instead (held longer)	
F f	qu in *quit*	V v	o in *note*	
D d	ks in *socks*	Ē ē	i in *sit*	
P p	f in *fan*	A a	o in *omit*	
M m	p in *pit*	Ī ī	ey in *obey*	
R r	s in *sit*	O o	a in *idea*	
X x	c in *cat*	Ā ā	a in *father*	
K k	k in *king*	L l	u in *rule*	
C c	m in *man*	Ū ū	l in *land*	
S s	r in *run*	E e	u in *put*	
N n	t in *tag*	H h	e in *bet*	
T t	n in *nut*	U u	h in *hat*	

Latin Workbook - Level 4
Copyright © 2000 by Karen Mohs

LATIN PRONUNCIATION REVIEW

Write the Latin letters for each sound.

1. Latin _____ sounds like **ph** in *phone*.

2. Latin _____ sounds like **oy** in *joy*.

3. Latin _____ sounds like **y** in *youth*.

4. Latin _____ sounds like *pt*.

5. Latin _____ sounds like *aye*.

6. Latin _____ sounds like **o** in *note*.

7. Latin _____ sounds like **ow** in *now*.

8. Latin _____ sounds like **ei** in *neighbor*.

9. Latin _____ sounds like **a** in *idea*.

10. Latin _____ sounds like **th** in *thick*.

11. Latin _____ sounds like *ps*.

12. Latin _____ sounds like **uee** in *queen*.

13. Latin _____ sounds like **su** in *suave*.

14. Latin _____ sounds like *ay-oo* (in one syllable).

15. Latin _____ sounds like **ch** in *character*.

16. Latin _____ sounds like **gu** in *anguish*.

6

Latin Workbook - Level 4
Copyright © 2000 by Karen Mohs

Lesson 2

VOCABULARY REVIEW

puella
puellae (feminine)*
means
girl

Write **girl** in Latin.

Write **woman** in Latin.

fēmina
fēminae (feminine)
means
woman, wife

puer
puerī (masculine)
means
boy

Write **boy** in Latin.

Write **forest** in Latin.

silva
silvae (feminine)
means
forest

agricola
agricolae (masculine)
means
farmer

Write **farmer** in Latin.

Write **water** in Latin.

aqua
aquae (feminine)
means
water

*Learn the nominative form (i.e. puella) and the genitive form (i.e. puellae) of each noun. Also learn the gender (masculine, feminine, or neuter). Write both the nominative and the genitive forms.

☐ Flashcards - (Add the new cards. Check the box when you practice your flashcards.)
(See the back of this workbook for the flashcards.)

Latin Workbook - Level 4
Copyright © 2000 by Karen Mohs

7

VOCABULARY REVIEW

est

means

he is, she is, it is, there is

Write **he is** in Latin.

Write **not** in Latin.

nōn

means

not

et

means

and, also, even

Write **and** in Latin.

Write **toward** in Latin.

ad

means

to, near, toward, for, at

īnsula
īnsulae (feminine)
means
island

Write **island** in Latin.

Write **they are** in Latin.

sunt

means

they are, there are

☐ Flashcards - (Add the new cards.)

8

Latin Workbook - Level 4
Copyright © 2000 by Karen Mohs

VOCABULARY REVIEW

laudō
laudāre laudāvī laudātum*
means
I praise

Write **I praise** in Latin.

Write **I call** in Latin.

vocō
vocāre vocāvī vocātum
means
I call

dō
dare dedī datum
means
I give, I grant

Write **I give** in Latin.

Write **life** in Latin.

vīta
vītae (feminine)
means
life

porta
portae (feminine)
means
gate

Write **gate** in Latin.

Write **memory** in Latin.

memoria
memoriae (feminine)
means
memory

*Learn all four principal parts of each verb. See page 39. Write all four principal parts.

☐ Flashcards - (Add the new cards.)

Latin Workbook - Level 4
Copyright © 2000 by Karen Mohs

9

VOCABULARY REVIEW

nāvigō
nāvigāre nāvigāvī nāvigātum
means
I sail

Write **I sail** in Latin.

Write **but** in Latin.

sed
means
but

fortūna
fortūnae (feminine)
means
fortune, chance, luck

Write **fortune** in Latin.

Write **road** in Latin.

via
viae (feminine)
means
road, way, street

portō
portāre portāvī portātum
means
I carry

Write **I carry** in Latin.

Write **what?** in Latin.

quid
means
what?

☐ Flashcards - (Add the new cards.)

10

Latin Workbook - Level 4
Copyright © 2000 by Karen Mohs

VOCABULARY REVIEW

tuba
tubae (feminine)
means
trumpet

Write **trumpet** in Latin.

Write **territory** in Latin.

ager
agrī (masculine)
means
field, territory

parō
parāre parāvī parātum
means
I prepare, I prepare for

Write **I prepare** in Latin.

Write **friend** in Latin.

amīcus
amīcī (masculine)
means
friend

spectō
spectāre spectāvī spectātum
means
I look at

Write **I look at** in Latin.

Write **nature** in Latin.

nātūra
nātūrae (feminine)
means
nature

☐ Flashcards - (Add the new cards.)

Latin Workbook - Level 4
Copyright © 2000 by Karen Mohs

11

Lesson 3

VOCABULARY REVIEW

campus
campī (masculine)
means
field, plain

Write **plain** in Latin.

Write **I seize** in Latin.

occupō
occupāre occupāvī occupātum
means
I seize, I capture

cum
means
along with, with

Write **along with** in Latin.

Write **sailor** in Latin.

nauta
nautae (masculine)
means
sailor

vīlla
vīllae (feminine)
means
farmhouse, country house, villa

Write **farmhouse** in Latin.

Write **letter** in Latin.

littera
litterae (feminine)
means
letter (of the alphabet),
(if plural: **epistle, letter**)

☐ Flashcards - (Add the new cards.)

12

Latin Workbook - Level 4
Copyright © 2000 by Karen Mohs

VOCABULARY REVIEW

ubi

means

where?

Write **where?** in Latin.

Write **son** in Latin.

filius

filī (masculine)

means

son

patria

patriae (feminine)

means

country, native land

Write **country** in Latin.

Write **daughter** in Latin.

filia

filiae (feminine)

means

daughter

amīcitia

amīcitiae (feminine)

means

friendliness, friendship

Write **friendship** in Latin.

Write **I love** in Latin.

amō

amāre amāvī amātum

means

I love, I like

☐ Flashcards - (Add the new cards.)

Latin Workbook - Level 4
Copyright © 2000 by Karen Mohs

13

VOCABULARY REVIEW

lingua
linguae (feminine)
means
tongue, language

Write **language** in Latin.

Write **horse** in Latin.

equus
equī (masculine)
means
horse

poēta
poētae (masculine)
means
poet

Write **poet** in Latin.

Write **year** in Latin.

annus
annī (masculine)
means
year

pugnō
pugnāre pugnāvī pugnātum
means
I fight

Write **I fight** in Latin.

Write **earth** in Latin.

terra
terrae (feminine)
means
earth, land, country

☐ Flashcards - (Add the new cards.)

14

Latin Workbook - Level 4
Copyright © 2000 by Karen Mohs

VOCABULARY REVIEW

gladius
gladī (masculine)
means
sword

Write **sword** in Latin.

Write **province** in Latin.

prōvincia
prōvinciae (feminine)
means
province

lēgātus
lēgātī (masculine)
means
lieutenant, ambassador, envoy

Write **lieutenant** in Latin.

Write **school** in Latin.

lūdus
lūdī (masculine)
means
game, play, school

appellō
appellāre appellāvī appellātum
means
I address, I call, I name

Write **I address** in Latin.

Write **slave** in Latin.

servus
servī (masculine)
means
slave

☐ Flashcards - (Add the new cards.)

Latin Workbook - Level 4
Copyright © 2000 by Karen Mohs

15

VOCABULARY REVIEW

nūntius
nūntī (masculine)
means
messenger, message, news

Write **messenger** in Latin.

Write **I announce** in Latin.

nūntiō
nūntiāre nūntiāvī nūntiātum
means
I announce, I report

nārrō
nārrāre nārrāvī nārrātum
means
I relate, I tell

Write **I tell** in Latin.

Write **reputation** in Latin.

fāma
fāmae (feminine)
means
report, rumor, reputation

populus*
populī (masculine)
means
people, nation, tribe

Write **tribe** in Latin.

Write **queen** in Latin.

rēgīna
rēgīnae (feminine)
means
queen

*Populus is usually singular. If plural, it means *nations* or *tribes*.

☐ Flashcards - (Add the new cards.)

16

Lesson 4

VOCABULARY REVIEW

exspectō
exspectāre exspectāvī exspectātum
means
I await, I wait for

Write **I wait for** in Latin.

Write **epistle** in Latin.

epistula
epistulae (feminine)
means
letter, epistle

habitō
habitāre habitāvī habitātum
means
I live, I dwell

Write **I live** in Latin.

Write **now** in Latin.

nunc

means

now

fābula
fābulae (feminine)
means
story

Write **story** in Latin.

Write **I please** in Latin.

dēlectō
dēlectāre dēlectāvī dēlectātum
means
I please

☐ Flashcards - (Add the new cards.)

Latin Workbook - Level 4
Copyright © 2000 by Karen Mohs

17

VOCABULARY REVIEW

labōrō
labōrāre labōrāvī labōrātum
means
**I labor, I suffer,
I am hard pressed**

Write **I am hard pressed** in Latin.

Write **reason** in Latin.

causa
causae (feminine)
means
cause, reason

socius
socī (masculine)
means
comrade, ally

Write **comrade** in Latin.

Write **diligence** in Latin.

dīligentia
dīligentiae (feminine)
means
diligence, care

convocō
convocāre convocāvī convocātum
means
**I call together,
I assemble, I summon**

Write **I assemble** in Latin.

Write **I surpass** in Latin.

superō
superāre superāvī superātum
means
I surpass, I defeat

☐ Flashcards - (Add the new cards.)

18

Latin Workbook - Level 4
Copyright © 2000 by Karen Mohs

VOCABULARY REVIEW

cōpia
cōpiae (feminine)
means
plenty, supply
(if plural: **troops, forces**)

Write **supply** in Latin.

Write **against** in Latin.

in
means
into, against, in, on

oppugnō
oppugnāre oppugnāvī oppugnātum
means
I attack

Write **I attack** in Latin.

Write **for a long time** in Latin.

diū
means
for a long time, long

vulnerō
vulnerāre vulnerāvī vulnerātum
means
I wound

Write **I wound** in Latin.

Write **exile** in Latin.

fuga
fugae (feminine)
means
flight, exile

□ Flashcards - (Add the new cards.)

Latin Workbook - Level 4
Copyright © 2000 by Karen Mohs

19

VOCABULARY REVIEW

iam

means

now, already

Write **already** in Latin.

Write **I attempt** in Latin.

temptō
temptāre temptāvī temptātum
means
I try, I attempt

herī

means

yesterday

Write **yesterday** in Latin.

Write **I guard** in Latin.

servō
servāre servāvī servātum
means
I guard, I save, I keep

poena
poenae (feminine)
means
penalty, punishment

Write **punishment** in Latin.

Write **always** in Latin.

semper

means

always

☐ Flashcards - (Add the new cards.)

20

Latin Workbook - Level 4
Copyright © 2000 by Karen Mohs

VOCABULARY REVIEW

captīvus
captīvī (masculine)
means
captive, prisoner

Write **captive** in Latin.

Write **location** in Latin.

locus
locī (masculine)
means
place, location, situation

audācia
audāciae (feminine)
means
boldness, daring

Write **boldness** in Latin.

Write **today** in Latin.

hodiē
means
today

volō
volāre volāvī volātum
means
I fly

Write **I fly** in Latin.

Write **mind** in Latin.

animus
animī (masculine)
means
mind, spirit
(if plural: **courage**)

☐ Flashcards - (Add the new cards.)

Latin Workbook - Level 4
Copyright © 2000 by Karen Mohs

21

Lesson 5

VOCABULARY REVIEW

crās

means

tomorrow

Write **tomorrow** in Latin.

Write **wagon** in Latin.

carrus
carrī (masculine)
means
cart, wagon

cūra
cūrae (feminine)
means
care, anxiety

Write **anxiety** in Latin.

Write **I stand** in Latin.

stō
stāre stetī stātum
means
I stand

saepe

means

often

Write **often** in Latin.

Write **I set free** in Latin.

līberō
līberāre līberāvī līberātum
means
I set free, I free

☐ Flashcards - (Add the new cards.)

22

Latin Workbook - Level 4
Copyright © 2000 by Karen Mohs

VOCABULARY REVIEW

interim

means

meanwhile

Write **meanwhile** in Latin.

Write **why?** in Latin.

cūr

means

why?

dēmōnstrō
dēmōnstrāre dēmōnstrāvī dēmōnstrātum
means
I point out, I show

Write **I point out** in Latin.

Write **hour** in Latin.

hōra
hōrae (feminine)
means
hour

posteā

means

**after that time,
afterward, thereafter**

Write **after that time** in Latin.

Write **poverty** in Latin.

inopia
inopiae (feminine)
means
want, lack, need, poverty

☐ Flashcards - (Add the new cards.)

Latin Workbook - Level 4
Copyright © 2000 by Karen Mohs

23

VOCABULARY REVIEW

pecūnia
pecūniae (feminine)
means
wealth, money

Write **wealth** in Latin.

Write **I strengthen** in Latin.

cōnfirmō
cōnfirmāre cōnfirmāvī cōnfirmātum
means
**I strengthen,
I encourage, I declare**

tum

means

then, at that time

Write **at that time** in Latin.

Write **I shout** in Latin.

clāmō
clāmāre clāmāvī clāmātum
means
I shout

dominus
dominī (masculine)
means
master, lord, owner

Write **owner** in Latin.

Write **I stroll** in Latin.

ambulō
ambulāre ambulāvī ambulātum
means
I stroll, I walk

☐ Flashcards - (Add the new cards.)

24

Latin Workbook - Level 4
Copyright © 2000 by Karen Mohs

VOCABULARY REVIEW

male

means

badly, insufficiently

Write **insufficiently** in Latin.

Write **number** in Latin.

numerus
numerī (masculine)
means
number, group

Circle **yes** or **no**.

yes   no   1. Parō is a Latin word that means **I prepare for**.

yes   no   2. Campus is a Latin word that means **territory**.

yes   no   3. Ubi is a Latin word that means **trumpet**.

yes   no   4. Pugnō is a Latin word that means **I fight**.

yes   no   5. Lēgātus is a Latin word that means **envoy**.

yes   no   6. Populus is a Latin word that means **people**.

yes   no   7. Fābula is a Latin word that means **story**.

yes   no   8. Superō is a Latin word that means **I fly**.

yes   no   9. Temptō is a Latin word that means **I beat**.

yes   no   10. Semper is a Latin word that means **always**.

yes   no   11. Carrus is a Latin word that means **anxiety**.

yes   no   12. Hōra is a Latin word that means **fear**.

☐ Flashcards - (Add the new cards.)

Latin Workbook - Level 4
Copyright © 2000 by Karen Mohs

VOCABULARY REVIEW

Match the words to their meanings.

sunt	I defeat	nūntius	need
superō	I await	lūdus	news
exspectō	there are	inopia	today
amō	I capture	hodiē	play
volō	I call	sed	year
occupō	I fly	annus	but
servō	I love	interim	at that time
vocō	I save	dīligentia	care
nāvigō	I encourage	porta	long
oppugnō	I attack	tum	meanwhile
cōnfirmō	I sail	cum	gate
stō	I stand	diū	along with
nārrō	I shout	ager	friendliness
clāmō	I try	male	insufficiently
appellō	I relate	et	tomorrow
temptō	I please	amīcitia	territory
dēlectō	I set free	crās	even
laudō	I address	posteā	farmer
liberō	I look at	agricola	thereafter
spectō	I praise	terra	earth

☐ Flashcards

26

Latin Workbook - Level 4
Copyright © 2000 by Karen Mohs

Lesson 6

DO YOU REMEMBER?

amō means **I like.**   amāmus means **We like.**

amās means **You** (singular) **like.**   amātis means **You** (plural) **like.**

amat means **He (she, it) likes.**   amant means **They like.**

This conjugation is called the *first conjugation - present active indicative*.

Match the words to their meanings.

ambulātis   you stroll

ambulat   I stroll

ambulō   she strolls

vulnerās   they wound

vulnerant   you wound

vulnerāmus   we wound

labōrō   you suffer

labōrātis   they suffer

labōrant   I suffer

dēmōnstrat   we show

dēmōnstrās   you show

dēmōnstrāmus   it shows

convocant   I summon

convocat   they summon

convocō   he summons

☐ Flashcards - (Add the new card.)

Latin Workbook - Level 4
Copyright © 2000 by Karen Mohs

27

LET'S PRACTICE

Circle the correct words.

he calls	I sail	you set free
vocant	nāvigātis	līberant
vocat	nāvigāmus	līberat
vocās	nāvigō	līberātis
you look at	**they fly**	**we like**
spectās	volātis	amāmus
spectō	volat	amātis
spectāmus	volant	amās
you announce	**she fights**	**I praise**
nūntiant	pugnant	laudās
nūntiātis	pugnat	laudat
nūntiō	pugnās	laudō
they try	**we guard**	**you name**
temptat	servāmus	appellās
temptātis	servātis	appellat
temptant	servant	appellāmus
I attack	**you seize**	**it pleases**
oppugnātis	occupō	dēlectās
oppugnō	occupāmus	dēlectat
oppugnāmus	occupātis	dēlectant
we carry	**you prepare**	**they await**
portāmus	parāmus	exspectat
portās	parās	exspectāmus
portant	parat	exspectant

☐ Flashcards

28

Latin Workbook - Level 4
Copyright © 2000 by Karen Mohs

Lesson 7

DO YOU REMEMBER?

Amat means **He likes.**

First Declension	Second Declension -ius	Second Declension -us
Puellam amat.	**Fīlium amat.**	**Amīcum amat.**
He likes *the girl*.	**He likes *the son*.**	**He likes *the friend*.**
Puellās amat.	**Fīliōs amat.**	**Amīcōs amat.**
He likes *the girls*.	**He likes *the sons*.**	**He likes *the friends*.**

Puellam, puellās, fīlium, fīliōs, amīcum, and amīcōs are in the Latin *accusative* case.
Words in this case are called *direct objects* in English grammar.

Write the correct Latin words in these sentences.

1. _____

   It means **He strengthens the spirit.**

2. _____

   It means **They carry swords.**

3. _____

   It means **You defeat the sailors.**

4. _____

   It means **They love the wives.**

5. _____

   It means **I give the horse.**

amant

animum

cōnfirmat

dō

equum

fēminās

gladiōs

nautās

portant

superātis

☐ Flashcards

Latin Workbook - Level 4
Copyright © 2000 by Karen Mohs

29

DO YOU REMEMBER?

Portam amat means **He likes the gate.**

First Declension	Second Declension -ius	Second Declension -us
Portam puellae amat.	**Portam filī amat.**	**Portam amīcī amat.**

First Declension	Second Declension -ius	Second Declension -us

Portam puellae amat.

He likes the gate *of the girl.*

or

He likes the *girl's* **gate.**

(The new ending, -ae, replaces the -a at the end of words like puella to show that the gate belongs to the girl.)

Portam filī amat.

He likes the gate *of the son.*

or

He likes the *son's* **gate.**

(The new ending, -ī, replaces the -ius at the end of words like filius [or the -us at the end of words like amīcus] to show that the gate belongs to the son [or to the friend].)

Portam amīcī amat.

He likes the gate *of the friend.*

or

He likes the *friend's* **gate.**

Portam puellārum amat.

He likes the gate *of the girls.*

or

He likes the *girls'* **gate.**

(The new ending, -ārum, replaces the -a at the end of words like puella to show that the gate belongs to **more than one** girl.)

Portam filiōrum* amat.

He likes the gate *of the sons.*

or

He likes the *sons'* **gate.**

(The new ending, -ōrum, replaces the -us at the end of words like filius or amīcus to show that the gate belongs to **more than one** son [or to **more than one** friend].

Portam amīcōrum amat.

He likes the gate *of the friends.*

or

He likes the *friends'* **gate.**

Puellae, puellārum, filī, filiōrum, amīcī, and amīcōrum are in the Latin *genitive* case.
The genitive case shows *possession*.

Circle the correct meaning of this Latin sentence.

Nūntium rēginae clāmō.	I shout the queen's message. I shout the queens' message. I shout the queen's messages.

*Careful! Unlike the singular -ius words, these plural possessive forms retain the -i- before the ending.

☐ Flashcards

DO YOU REMEMBER?

Puellam amat means **He likes the girl.**

Who is *he*?

First Declension	Second Declension -ius	Second Declension -us
Agricola puellam amat.	Fīlius puellam amat.	Amīcus puellam amat.
The farmer likes the girl.	*The son* likes the girl.	*The friend* likes the girl.
Agricolae puellam amant.	Fīliī puellam amant.	Amīcī puellam amant.
The farmers like the girl.	*The sons* like the girl.	*The friends* like the girl.

(Sometimes endings for different uses have the same spelling. On page 30, we learned that the -ae ending can indicate possession. Here we learn that the same -ae ending can be a plural subject.)

(Notice that the words ending in -ius retain the -i- of the base when meaning more than one, as in fīliī. As we learned on page 30, the -i- in singular words is dropped when indicating possession.)

Agricola, agricolae, fīlius, fīliī, amīcus, and amīcī are in the Latin ***nominative*** case. Words in this case are called ***subjects*** in English grammar.

Write the meanings of the Latin sentences on the lines beneath the sentences.

Īnsulam spectat. _____	Carrum servī laudās. _____
Lēgātus īnsulam spectat. _____	Poētae carrum servī laudant. _____
Fīlium portat. _____	Populum līberant. _____
Agricola fīlium portat. _____	Sociī populum līberant. _____

☐ Flashcards

Latin Workbook - Level 4
Copyright © 2000 by Karen Mohs

31

LET'S PRACTICE

Write the Latin words to complete the sentences. Write their meanings.

1. Fīlī amīcus nūntium _____ exspectat.
   (of the native land)

   It means _____

2. Tubam _____ laudat.
   (of the master)

   It means _____

3. Posteā _____ inopiam prōvinciae dēmōnstrant.
   (the prisoners)

   It means _____

4. Pecūnia _____ nōn saepe dēlectat.
   (the poet)

   It means _____

5. Vīllae _____ nunc stant.
   (of the sailors)

   It means _____

6. Interim fīliī numerum _____ superant.
   (of envoys)

   It means _____

7. Agricolae _____ aquam et gladium portat.
   (the daughter)

   It means _____

☐ Flashcards

DO YOU REMEMBER?

Word Order

Word order in Latin is not the same as word order in English.

English	**Latin**
The *position* of the word tells what role the word plays in the sentence.	The *ending* of the word tells what role the word plays in the sentence.
Normal word order: SUBJECT - VERB - DIRECT OBJECT	Normal word order: Most important word (usually the verb) is often *last*. Second most important word is often *first*. (Note: If the verb is a linking verb, the Latin word order usually follows the English word order.)

Write the sentences in Latin, giving two different word orders for each one.

1. The boy loves the master.

    a. _____

    b. _____

2. The farmer tells the story.

    a. _____

    b. _____

3. The girl waits for the daughter.

    a. _____

    b. _____

☐ Flashcards

Latin Workbook - Level 4
Copyright © 2000 by Karen Mohs

DO YOU REMEMBER?

Carrum dō means **I give the cart.**

First Declension	Second Declension -ius	Second Declension -us
Puellae carrum dō.	Filiō carrum dō.	Amīcō carrum dō.
I give the cart *to the girl.*	**I give the cart** *to the son.*	**I give the cart** *to the friend.*
or	or	or
I give the cart *for the girl.*	**I give the cart** *for the son.*	**I give the cart** *for the friend.*

(Notice that this ending, -ae, is identical to the endings of two other cases. See pages 30 and 31.)

Puellīs carrum dō.	Filiīs carrum dō.	Amīcīs carrum dō.
I give the cart *to the girls.*	**I give the cart** *to the sons.*	**I give the cart** *to the friends.*
or	or	or
I give the cart *for the girls.*	**I give the cart** *for the sons.*	**I give the cart** *for the friends.*

Puellae, puellīs, filiō, filiīs, amīcō, and amīcīs are in the Latin *dative* case.
Words in this case are called ***indirect objects*** in English grammar.

Put the correct endings on these Latin words.

at us ō um	1. The friend gives the sword to the son. Amīc_____ fili_____ gladi_____ d_____.	
am īs ant ae	2. The poets tell the story to the slaves. Poēt_____ serv_____ fābul_____ nārr_____.	
īs ae ās āmus	3. We carry the epistles to the farmer. Agricol_____ epistul_____ port_____.	

☐ Flashcards

34

Latin Workbook - Level 4
Copyright © 2000 by Karen Mohs

DO YOU REMEMBER?

Puella habitat means **The girl lives.**

Where does the girl live?

First Declension
In īnsulā puella habitat.
The girl lives
on the island.

Second Declension
In lūdō puella habitat.
The girl lives
in the school.

(Notice that this singular ending, -ō, is identical to the singular ending of another noun case. See page 34.)

In īnsulīs puella habitat.
The girl lives
on the islands.

In lūdīs puella habitat.
The girl lives
in the schools.

(Notice that this plural ending, -īs, is identical to the plural ending of another noun case. See page 34.)

Īnsulā, īnsulīs, lūdō, and lūdīs are in the Latin *ablative* case.
In this Latin construction, ***Ablative of Place Where***,
the preposition in is used with the ablative case.

Match the Latin sentences to their meanings.

_____ 1. Locus puellam pugnat.

_____ 2. In locō puellās pugnāmus.

_____ 3. In locīs puellam pugnāmus.

_____ 4. Locus puellās pugnat.

_____ 5. Puellam in locō pugnat.

a. It fights the girl in the place.

b. The place fights the girls.

c. We fight the girl in the places.

d. The place fights the girl.

e. We fight the girls in the place.

☐ Flashcards

Latin Workbook - Level 4
Copyright © 2000 by Karen Mohs

35

DO YOU REMEMBER?

Puellās convocō means **I summon the girls.**

By what *means* do I summon the girls?

First Declension

Puellās tubā convocō.

I summon the girls with (*by means of*) the trumpet.

Second Declension

Puellās nūntiō convocō.

I summon the girls with (*by means of*) the message.

(As the student translates, he may use any of a number of prepositions [**with**, **in**, **on**, etc.],
but he must remember that the idea of this construction is *by means of*.)

Puellās tubīs convocō.

I summon the girls with (*by means of*) the trumpets.

Puellās nūntiīs convocō.

I summon the girls with (*by means of*) the messages.

Tubā, tubīs, nūntiō, and nūntiīs are in the Latin *ablative* case.
In this Latin construction, *Ablative of Means or Instrument*,
the ablative case is used without a preposition.

Circle the correct words.

with the sword	in the province	with horses
gladium	in prōvinciā	in equīs
gladiīs	in prōvinciae	equō
gladiō	in prōvinciīs	equīs
by means of gates	with money	in the field
in portīs	pecūnia	in campō
portīs	pecūniā	in campus
in portō	pecūniārum	in campī

☐ Flashcards

36

Latin Workbook - Level 4
Copyright © 2000 by Karen Mohs

DO YOU REMEMBER?

Pugnō means **I fight.**

In what *manner* do I fight?

First Declension

Cum audāciā pugnō.
I fight *with boldness.*

(As the student translates, he may use the preposition **with**, but he must remember
that the idea of this construction is the *manner* in which a thing is done.)

Audāciā is in the Latin *ablative* case.
In this Latin construction, ***Ablative of Manner,***
the preposition cum is used with the ablative case.

Write the correct Latin words on the lines beside the meanings.

in the farmhouses _____

with anxiety _____

in the situation _____

on the islands _____

with the message _____

with friendliness _____

on the horse _____

with the swords _____

with daring _____

☐ Flashcards - (Add the new cards. These new cards contain the forms reviewed on pages 29-37.)

Latin Workbook - Level 4
Copyright © 2000 by Karen Mohs

LET'S PRACTICE

Choose the best words for the sentences below. Put them in the blanks.
Write what the sentences mean.

audācia	silvā	lēgātō

1. Captīvī fāmās in lūdō et in _____ clāmant.

   It means _____

2. _____ poenam hodiē et crās nārrāmus.

   It means _____

3. Puer cum _____ causam fugae dēmōnstrat.

   It means _____

terrās	terrārum	terrā

1. In _____ habitō, sed nōn amō prōvinciam.

   It means _____

2. Silvās _____ fīliārum rēgīnae spectās.

   It means _____

3. Cūr _____ et agricolās sociōrum oppugnātis?

   It means _____

☐ Flashcards

38

Latin Workbook - Level 4
Copyright © 2000 by Karen Mohs

Lesson 8

PRINCIPAL PARTS OF VERBS

Latin verbs generally have four main **parts**, called *principal parts*.

The Principal Parts of the Verb Amō

amō   amāre   amāvī   amātum

These principal parts contain the **stems** which are so important to Latin grammar. Endings are added to these stems to create a large variety of verb forms.

Look at the **first** principal part, amō. This is the part most dictionaries use to list the word.

Look at the **second** principal part, amāre. Remove -re and you will have the *present stem*. If the present stem ends in -ā, the verb is a *first conjugation verb*. The principal parts of all regular first conjugation verbs have the same endings. These endings are -ō, -āre, -āvī, and -ātum. (All verbs you have learned so far, with the exception of sum, stō, and dō,* are regular first conjugation verbs.)

(We will learn the uses of the **third** and **fourth** principal parts
in future workbooks of this series.)

Add the missing endings to these first conjugation principal parts.

am____   am_____   am_____   am_____

voc____   voc_____   voc_____   voc_____

serv____   serv_____   serv_____   serv_____

par____   par_____   par_____   par_____

*The principal parts of sum are sum, esse, fuī, and futūrus. (As we have learned, the principal parts of dō are dō, dare, dedī, and datum, and the principal parts of stō are stō, stāre, stetī, and statum.)

☐ Flashcards - (Add the new card.)

Latin Workbook - Level 4
Copyright © 2000 by Karen Mohs

39

LET'S PRACTICE

Write the words on the right under the correct headings.

first principal part

second principal part

third principal part

fourth principal part

amātum
ambulāre
appellāre
clāmātum
cōnfirmāvī
convocō
dēlectō
dēmōnstrō
exspectō
labōrāvī
laudāre
līberāvī
nārrāvī
nāvigāre
nūntiātum
occupāre
parō
portātum
pugnātum
superāre
temptāvī
vocō
volāvī
vulnerātum

☐ Flashcards

40

Latin Workbook - Level 4
Copyright © 2000 by Karen Mohs

Lesson 9

MACRONS

A macron is a horizontal line which is placed above a vowel to show that the vowel is long. When pronounced, a vowel with a macron is held twice as long as a vowel without a macron.

The Romans did not use macrons. Latin grammar books often use them to aid in teaching the length of the vowels. It is important to learn the placement of macrons when learning the spelling of a word.

Certain special rules govern the use of macrons.

A vowel **always** has a macron before the letters -ns.

vocāns   regēns

A vowel **never** has a macron before the letters -nt.

amant   spectantur

In most fifth declension* words, when the vowel -e- comes after another vowel, it has a macron.

diēī   speī

When an -m, -r, or -t is the last letter in an ending added to a word, the vowel that comes before the -m, -r, or -t is **never** long.

vocābam   vocābar   vocābat

If an -m, -r, or -t is the last letter in a word without an ending, the vowel that comes before the -m, -r, or -t is *almost* **never** long.

cum   semper   et

(Cūr is one of the exceptions.)

Cross out the Latin words with incorrect macrons.

appellat	habitāns	superābār	tum	dēlectābām
servans	diebus	speī	oppugnānt	labōrat
laudābar	spectant	monēns	diēs	sempēr
ambulābam	portāt	nārrānt	clāmāt	nāvigant

*You will learn the fifth declension beginning on page 131.

☐ Flashcards - (Add the new cards.)

Latin Workbook - Level 4
Copyright © 2000 by Karen Mohs

41

LET'S PRACTICE

Choose the correct words for the sentences. Put them in the blanks.
Write what the sentences mean.

equis - equīs

1. _____ aquam dō.

It means _____

vīlla - vīllā

2. In _____ agricolae habitāmus.

It means _____

campo - campō

3. Nautae amīcus est in _____.

It means _____

portant - portānt

4. Lēgātī gladiōs et epistulās _____.

It means _____

servant - servānt

5. Captīvī in prōvinciā _____ amīcōs servōrum.

It means _____

laudat - laudāt

6. Interim fēmina memoriam puellae _____.

It means _____

cur - cūr

7. _____ nautārum filiae carrum amant?

It means _____

☐ Flashcards

42

Latin Workbook - Level 4
Copyright © 2000 by Karen Mohs

NAMES OF SYLLABLES

Before we learn the **Rules of Accent**, we must know the names of the last three syllables of Latin words.

1. The last syllable is the **ultima**.
2. The syllable before the ultima is the **penult**.
3. The syllable before the penult is the **antepenult**.

e   pis   tu   la

antepenult   penult   ultima

Write *penult*, *ultima*, or *antepenult* on the lines beneath the syllables.

nā   vi   gā   mus

_____ _____ _____ _____

op   pug   nat

_____ _____ _____

prō   vin   ci   ās

_____ _____ _____ _____

cōn   fir   mā   tis

_____ _____ _____ _____

au   dā   ci   ā

_____ _____ _____ _____

pe   cū   ni   am

_____ _____ _____ _____

vul   ne   rō

_____ _____ _____

☐ Flashcards - (Add the new card.)

Latin Workbook - Level 4
Copyright © 2000 by Karen Mohs

DIVISION OF SYLLABLES

Rules for Dividing Syllables

A Latin word has as many syllables as it has vowels or diphthongs.
Separate vowels that are next to other vowels or diphthongs.
Examples: vi' a   pa' tri ae   fi' li ō   prō vin' ci ae

When a consonant stands between two vowels or diphthongs:
Pronounce the consonant in the syllable with the second vowel or diphthong.
Examples: po' pu lus   rē gī' nae   fā' bu la   cau' sae

When two or more consonants stand between two vowels or diphthongs:
Pronounce only the last consonant in the syllable with the second vowel or diphthong.
Examples: temp' tō   cap tī' vus   for tū' na   an' nus
(Certain consonants like to stay together, such as h, l, or r coming after c, g, p, b, d, or t.)
Examples: pa' tri a   am' plus   a grī' co la   ac clā' mō

When the consonant is a double consonant* (x or z):
Place -x- with the vowel before, but -z- with the vowel after.
Examples: ux' or   sax' um   gā' za   ci tha' ri zō

When the word is compound:
Separate the prefix from the rest of the word.
Examples: ex spec' tō   con' vo cō   sub ti' me ō   in dū' cō

Divide the words correctly by drawing vertical lines between the syllables.

campus	labōrō	cōpia	ambulō
amīcitia	gladius	fāma	nūntiō
dīligentia	dēmōnstrō	appellō	occupō

*The letters x and z are called double consonants because two sounds are needed to pronounce them. Pronounce the initial sound with the first syllable and the final sound with the second syllable.

□ Flashcards - (Add the new cards.)

44
Latin Workbook - Level 4
Copyright © 2000 by Karen Mohs

LENGTH OF SYLLABLES

Syllables can be *long by nature* or *long by position*.

Syllables which are *long by nature*:
1. A syllable is long by nature if it contains a long vowel (a vowel with a macron over it).
   Example: -dō in laudō is a long syllable.

2. A syllable is long by nature if it contains a diphthong.
   Example: lau- in laudō is a long syllable.

Syllables which are *long by position*:
1. A syllable is long by position if its vowel is followed by two or more consonants.
   Example: pug- in pugnō is a long syllable.

2. A syllable is long by position if its vowel is followed by a double consonant (-x or -z).
   Example: ux- in uxor is a long syllable.

Circle the correct words.

1. In the word superō, the syllable su- is (short, long) and is called the (antepenult, penult, ultima).

2. In the word semper, the syllable sem- is (short, long) and is called the (antepenult, penult, ultima).

3. In the word posteā, the syllable -te- is (short, long) and is called the (antepenult, penult, ultima).

4. In the word habitō, the syllable -tō is (short, long) and is called the (antepenult, penult, ultima).

☐ Flashcards - (Add the new cards.)

Latin Workbook - Level 4
Copyright © 2000 by Karen Mohs

LET'S PRACTICE

Write the words on the right under the correct headings. (Most words will be used more than once.)

short antepenult

long antepenult

| dēlectō |
| dominō |
| inopia |
| lēgātī |
| nātūra |
| nōn |
| poēta |
| stō |
| ubi |
| via |

short penult

long penult

short ultima

long ultima

☐ Flashcards

46

Latin Workbook - Level 4
Copyright © 2000 by Karen Mohs

RULES OF ACCENT

1. One syllable words:

   Accent the ultima (the only syllable).

   Examples: dō   cum   stō   est

2. Two syllable words:

   Accent the penult.

   Examples: a'ger   lin'gua   por'ta   u'bi

3. Three (or more) syllable words:

   Accent the penult if it is long (by nature or by position).

   Examples: po ē'ta   rē gī'na   pu el'la   ex spec'tō

   Accent the antepenult if the penult is short.

   Examples: su'pe rō   fē'mi na   me mo'ri a   ha'bi tō

Write **a** beside the words that should be accented on the ***antepenult***, **p** beside the words that should be accented on the ***penult***, and **u** beside the words that should be accented on the ***ultima***.

____ 1. aqua	____ 9. herī	____ 17. līberō	____ 25. terra
____ 2. appellō	____ 10. ad	____ 18. silva	____ 26. nūntius
____ 3. fuga	____ 11. poena	____ 19. numerus	____ 27. vocō
____ 4. fīlius	____ 12. nārrō	____ 20. est	____ 28. iam
____ 5. lūdus	____ 13. hodiē	____ 21. animus	____ 29. hōra
____ 6. dō	____ 14. socius	____ 22. īnsula	____ 30. et
____ 7. diū	____ 15. tuba	____ 23. fortūna	____ 31. portō
____ 8. vīta	____ 16. servus	____ 24. vīlla	____ 32. volō

☐ Flashcards - (Add the new cards.)

Latin Workbook - Level 4
Copyright © 2000 by Karen Mohs

LET'S PRACTICE

Write the words on the right under the correct headings.

accent the antepenult

accent the penult

accent the ultima

ambulō
animus
captīvus
cōnfirmō
cūr
dēlectō
dēmōnstrō
dominus
est
fēmina
gladius
in
inopia
īnsula
lingua
parō
portō
posteā
puella
saepe
sed
spectō
temptō
terra
vocō

☐ Flashcards

48

Latin Workbook - Level 4
Copyright © 2000 by Karen Mohs

Lesson 10

verbum
verbī (neuter)*
means
word

Write the Latin word that means **word**.

Write the Latin word that means **husband**.

vir
virī (masculine)
means
**man, husband,
hero**

caelum
caelī (neuter)
means
sky, heavens

Write the Latin word that means **sky**.

*Remember: Learn both the nominative form (i.e. **verbum**) and the genitive form (i.e. **verbī**) of each noun. Also learn the gender (masculine, feminine, or neuter). Remember to write the nominative and the genitive forms.

☐ Flashcards - (Add the new cards.)

Latin Workbook - Level 4
Copyright © 2000 by Karen Mohs

49

LET'S PRACTICE

Circle the Latin words to match the English meanings.

in the country	in patriā	in patria	in patriae
at that time	tuba	terra	tum
we try	temptat	temptās	temptāmus
of the horses	equōs	equōrum	equī
they relate	nārrant	nārrat	nārrātis
along with	cum	cūr	crās
for the wife	fēminā	fēminam	fēminae
husband	via	vir	vīlla
penalties	poenā	poenam	poenae
there are	sunt	est	et
you guard	servant	servāmus	servātis
word	vīta	verbum	vulnerō
of the gate	portae	portārum	portam
with the trumpet	tubā	tubam	tubae
she surpasses	superātis	superant	superat
stories	fābulā	fābulam	fābulās
often	semper	saepe	sed
you prepare	parās	parāmus	parat
groups	numerus	numerōrum	numerī
sky	cōpia	caelum	causa
with daring	cum audāciā	cum audāciae	cum audācia

☐ Flashcards

50

Latin Workbook - Level 4
Copyright © 2000 by Karen Mohs

rēx

rēgis (masculine)

means

king

Write the Latin word that means **king**.

Write the Latin word that means **I see**.

videō

vidēre vīdī vīsum*

means

I see

scrībō

scrībere scrīpsī scrīptum

means

I write

Write the Latin word that means **I write**.

*Remember: Learn all four principal parts of each verb. See page 39. Remember to write all four principal parts.

☐ Flashcards - (Add the new cards.)

Latin Workbook - Level 4
Copyright © 2000 by Karen Mohs

51

LET'S PRACTICE

Match the words to their meanings.

fāma	daughter
filius	rumor
filia	son
rēgina	now
nunc	king
rēx	queen
vir	street
vīta	life
via	hero
habitō	yesterday
herī	I dwell
hodiē	today
vocō	I call
vulnerō	I wound
videō	I see
caelum	word
verbum	heavens
ubi	where?
spectō	slave
servus	I write
scrībō	I look at

☐ Flashcards

52

Latin Workbook - Level 4
Copyright © 2000 by Karen Mohs

Lesson 11

gēns
gentis (feminine)
means
**nation, family,
clan**

Write the Latin word that means **clan**.

Write the Latin word that means **I tell**.

dīcō
dīcere dīxī dictum
means
I say, I tell

respondeō
respondēre respondī respōnsum
means
I answer, I reply

Write the Latin word that means **I answer**.

☐ Flashcards - (Add the new cards.)

Latin Workbook - Level 4
Copyright © 2000 by Karen Mohs

53

LET'S PRACTICE

Circle the correct words.

heavens	I see	I fly
carrus cōpia caelum	vulnerō videō vocō	nāvigō pugnō volō
forest	flight	family
socius silva superō	fuga fāma fortūna	gēns fīlia amīcus
I say	word	friendship
dēlectō dīcō dēmōnstrō	lingua epistula verbum	annus amīcitia audācia
after that time	I answer	letter
poēta patria posteā	respondeō exspectō līberō	lēgātus littera locus
king	need	husband
rēx rēgīna lūdus	inopia interim iam	vir vīta via
I write	field	number
spectō scrībō stō	animus agricola ager	numerus nunc nūntius

☐ Flashcards

54

Latin Workbook - Level 4
Copyright © 2000 by Karen Mohs

mare

maris (neuter)

means

sea

Write the Latin word that means **sea**.

_____

_____

_____

_____

_____

Write the Latin word that means **brother**.

_____

_____

_____

_____

_____

frāter

frātris (masculine)

means

brother

dūcō

dūcere dūxī ductum

means

I lead, I bring

Write the Latin word that means **I lead**.

_____

_____

_____

_____

_____

☐　Flashcards - (Add the new cards.)

Latin Workbook - Level 4
Copyright © 2000 by Karen Mohs

55

LET'S PRACTICE

Write the meanings of the following Latin words.

quid _____

dīcō _____

vir _____

diū _____

scrībō _____

semper _____

dūcō _____

verbum _____

hodiē _____

rēx _____

puella _____

mare _____

porta _____

gēns _____

frāter _____

oppugnō _____

caelum _____

saepe _____

crās _____

respondeō _____

ubi _____

male _____

videō _____

aqua _____

equus _____

☐ Flashcards

Lesson 12

urbs
urbis (feminine)
means
city

Write the Latin word that means **city**.

Write the Latin word that means **grain**.

frūmentum
frūmentī (neuter)
means
grain

soror
sorōris (feminine)
means
sister

Write the Latin word that means **sister**.

☐ Flashcards - (Add the new cards.)

Latin Workbook - Level 4
Copyright © 2000 by Karen Mohs

57

LET'S PRACTICE

Match the Latin words to their meanings.

_____	1. videō	a.	I report
_____	2. nūntiō	b.	I capture
_____	3. mare	c.	I bring
_____	4. occupō	d.	I say
_____	5. dīcō	e.	I see
_____	6. terra	f.	I attempt
_____	7. dūcō	g.	earth
_____	8. temptō	h.	sea
_____	9. rēx	i.	punishment
_____	10. vir	j.	I carry
_____	11. ambulō	k.	man
_____	12. portō	l.	heavens
_____	13. gēns	m.	I write
_____	14. caelum	n.	king
_____	15. poena	o.	nation
_____	16. scrībō	p.	I walk
_____	17. verbum	q.	province
_____	18. prōvincia	r.	I answer
_____	19. frāter	s.	care
_____	20. dīligentia	t.	word
_____	21. tum	u.	hour
_____	22. hōra	v.	I praise
_____	23. respondeō	w.	at that time
_____	24. laudō	x.	brother

☐ Flashcards

Latin Workbook - Level 4
Copyright © 2000 by Karen Mohs

hostis
hostis (masculine)

means

**enemy
(of the State)**

Write the Latin word that means **enemy**.

Write the Latin word that means **I remain**.

maneō
manēre mānsī mānsum

means

I stay, I remain

dēligō
dēligere dēlēgī dēlēctum

means

I choose

Write the Latin word that means **I choose**.

☐ Flashcards - (Add the new cards.)

Latin Workbook - Level 4
Copyright © 2000 by Karen Mohs

59

LET'S PRACTICE

Circle the correct words.

I tell	dō dūcō dīcō	I reply	oppugnō respondeō volō
boy	puer populus parō	I choose	clāmō dēligō nāvigō
I write	sunt servō scrībō	money	campus herī pecūnia
I suffer	appellō labōrō cōnfirmō	family	gēns cūra fēmina
I stay	amō maneō clāmō	enemy	captīvus hostis dominus
memory	nātūra vīlla memoria	brother	causa frāter nauta
sea	mare maneō male	I dwell	habitō convocō nārrō

☐ Flashcards

60

Latin Workbook - Level 4
Copyright © 2000 by Karen Mohs

Lesson 13

māter
mātris (feminine)

means

mother

Write the Latin word that means **mother**.

Write the Latin word that means **I sit**.

sedeō
sedēre sēdī sessum

means

I sit

mors
mortis (feminine)

means

death

Write the Latin word that means **death**.

☐ Flashcards - (Add the new cards.)

Latin Workbook - Level 4
Copyright © 2000 by Karen Mohs

61

LET'S PRACTICE

Circle the correct words.

word	enemy	hero
vīta vīlla verbum	poena hostis terra	vir socius puer
I stay	I tell	I choose
maneō occupō stō	parō laudō dīcō	superō dēligō servō
I sit	mother	sky
dēlectō sedeō ambulō	populus iam māter	caelum saepe vulnerō
clan	king	sea
gēns equus locus	fāma rēx dominus	mare diū hōra
brother	death	I see
carrus frāter fīlius	mors fuga crās	līberō amō videō
I answer	I lead	I write
exspectō respondeō appellō	habitō cōnfirmō dūcō	convocō nārrō scrībō

☐ Flashcards

62

Latin Workbook - Level 4
Copyright © 2000 by Karen Mohs

LET'S PRACTICE

Review the names of the cases on pages 29-37. Write the name of the **case** (nominative, genitive, dative, accusative, ablative) and the **number** (singular, plural) beside each Latin word.

	case	number			case	number
campus	_____	_____		campī	_____	_____
campī	_____	_____		campōrum	_____	_____
campō	_____	_____		campīs	_____	_____
campum	_____	_____		campōs	_____	_____
in campō	_____	_____		in campīs	_____	_____

Write the meanings beside the Latin words.

terra	_____	terrae	_____
terrae	_____	terrārum	_____
terrae	_____	terrīs	_____
terram	_____	terrās	_____
in terrā	_____	in terrīs	_____

gladius	_____	gladiī	_____
gladī	_____	gladiōrum	_____
gladiō	_____	gladiīs	_____
gladium	_____	gladiōs	_____
gladiō	_____	gladiīs	_____

☐ Flashcards

Latin Workbook - Level 4
Copyright © 2000 by Karen Mohs

63

LET'S PRACTICE

Write the meanings of the Latin words. On the last set, write the Latin words.

amō _____

amās _____

amat _____

amāmus _____

amātis _____

amant _____

parō _____

parās _____

parat _____

parāmus _____

parātis _____

parant _____

temptō _____

temptās _____

temptat _____

temptāmus _____

temptātis _____

temptant _____

nārrō _____

nārrās _____

nārrat _____

nārrāmus _____

nārrātis _____

nārrant _____

laudō _____

laudās _____

laudat _____

laudāmus _____

laudātis _____

laudant _____

clāmō _____

clāmās _____

clāmat _____

clāmāmus _____

clāmātis _____

clāmant _____

I fly _____

you (sing.) fly _____

he (she, it) flies _____

we fly _____

you (pl.) fly _____

they fly _____

☐ Flashcards

64

LET'S PRACTICE

Write these sentences in Latin.

1. I see the captives in the queen's province.

2. Why does the brother love the farmer's story?

3. I write the epistle to the woman and to the lieutenant.

4. The messenger shouts the rumor to the ally today.

5. I lead the slaves by means of the sword and the trumpet.

6. The man praises the poet with boldness.

7. Now the king in the forest points out the water.

☐ Flashcards

Latin Workbook - Level 4
Copyright © 2000 by Karen Mohs

65

PUZZLE TIME!

Write the correct Latin **principal part** as requested after the English meaning. That is, if (*first*) appears, write the first principal part in the puzzle, and so on.

across	down
2. walk (*third*)	1. defeat (*fourth*)
6. praise (*third*)	3. stay (*first*)
10. fight (*first*)	4. set free (*fourth*)
11. shout (*second*)	5. carry (*first*)
12. await (*second*)	7. please (*fourth*)
13. lead (*first*)	8. strengthen (*second*)
15. stand (*first*)	9. look at (*third*)
18. attempt (*fourth*)	13. give (*first*)
21. sail (*fourth*)	14. love (*fourth*)
22. fly (*second*)	15. write (*first*)
23. love (*third*)	16. see (*first*)
24. live (*fourth*)	17. relate (*first*)
25. love (*second*)	19. prepare for (*third*)
26. say (*first*)	20. call (*second*)
27. answer (*first*)	

☐ Flashcards

Lesson 14

SUM - THE "BEING" VERB

sum means **I am.** sumus means **We are.**

es means **You (singular) are.** estis means **You (plural) are.**

est means **He (she, it) is, there is.** sunt means **They are, there are.**

Use the forms of sum to "link" a subject (*nominative*) with another word in
the nominative case that renames the subject (*predicate nominative*).

Match the words and sentences to their meanings.

es   you (pl.) are

estis   he is

est   you (sing.) are

sumus   we are

sum   I am

sunt   they are

Sum puer.   You are the boy.

Es puer.   I am the boy.

Est puer.   He is the boy.

Estis puellae.   They are girls.

Sumus puellae.   You are girls.

Sunt puellae.   We are girls.

Sunt litterae.   The cart is on the island.

Est gladius.   There is the sword.

Carrus est in īnsulā.   There are letters.

☐ Flashcards - (Add the new card.)

Latin Workbook - Level 4
Copyright © 2000 by Karen Mohs

67

LET'S PRACTICE

Choose the correct words for the sentences. Put them in the blanks.
Write what the sentences mean.

sum - sumus

1. _____ rēx agricolārum nautārumque*.

It means _____

spectat - spectant

2. Fīliine** equōs _____?

It means _____

viae - viā

3. In _____ sedeō, sed nōn sum fīlia.

It means _____

poētam - poētā

4. Ubi frāter _____ nūntiumque pugnat?

It means _____

que - ne

5. Sunt _____ silvae in īnsulā rēgīnae?

It means _____

sociī - socius

6. Cum amīcitiā _____ captīvōs dēmōnstrant.

It means _____

*When you see -que at the end of a word, translate it "and" before the word on which it is attached. To use this connective, both words should play the same role in the sentence. (That is, both words should be subjects, or both should be direct objects, or both should be indirect objects, etc.)

**When you see -ne at the end of the first word in a sentence, the sentence should be translated as a question. Only use -ne when the question can be answered with *yes* or *no*.

☐ Flashcards

68

Latin Workbook - Level 4
Copyright © 2000 by Karen Mohs

Lesson 15

ABLATIVE OF ACCOMPANIMENT

Puella ambulat means **The girl walks.**

With whom does the girl walk?

First Declension
Cum fēminā
puella ambulat.
The girl walks
with the woman.

Second Declension
Cum amīcō
puella ambulat.
The girl walks
with the friend.

Cum fēminīs
puella ambulat.
The girl walks
with the women.

Cum amīcīs
puella ambulat.
The girl walks
with the friends.

In this Latin construction, *Ablative of Accompaniment*,
the preposition cum is used with the ablative case.

(Be careful not to confuse this with the *Ablative of Manner*, which also uses
the preposition cum with the ablative case. See page 37.)

Write the correct Latin words in these sentences.

1. _____

It means **The comrade lives with the son.**

2. _____

It means **The comrades live with the sons.**

3. _____

It means **The sons walk with the comrades.**

ambulant
cum filiīs
cum filiō
cum sociīs
filiī
habitant
habitat
sociī
socius

☐ Flashcards

Latin Workbook - Level 4
Copyright © 2000 by Karen Mohs

69

LET'S PRACTICE

Read these Latin sentences. Write what they mean.

1. Interim puella fābulās agricolae semper laudat.

   It means _____

2. Nautās lēgātōsque dūcō, sed pecūniam nōn amō.

   It means _____

3. Estisne fīliae amīcī rēgīnae?

   It means _____

4. Cūr agricolae cum servīs in lūdō habitant?

   It means _____

5. Cūra est, sed verbum dominī puellās cōnfīrmat.

   It means _____

6. Tum fēminīs servīsque captīvōrum epistulās scrībō.

   It means _____

7. Mors lēgātī poētās in prōvinciā dēlectat.

   It means _____

8. Vīllam spectō, sed animōs fīliōrum nōn videō.

   It means _____

9. Īnsulam oppugnant, et numerum nautārum tum occupant.

   It means _____

10. Quid est causa fortūnae dominī et inopiae servī?

    It means _____

☐ Flashcards

70

Latin Workbook - Level 4
Copyright © 2000 by Karen Mohs

Lesson 16

LATIN NOUNS - DECLENSION

Latin nouns are grouped according to their *declension*.*

First declension:

These nouns are usually *feminine* (but sometimes *masculine*) in gender.

They end with -ae in their **genitive** (possessive) **singular case**.

Examples** (feminine): puella aqua nātūra

Examples (masculine): agricola nauta poēta

Second declension:

These nouns are usually *masculine* or *neuter* in gender.

They end with -ī in their **genitive** (possessive) **singular case**.

Examples*** (masculine): amīcus fīlius puer

Examples (neuter): verbum caelum

(We will learn about the **third**, **fourth**, and **fifth** declensions later.)

Write the words on the right under the correct headings.

first declension feminine

second declension masculine

first declension masculine

second declension neuter

ager
caelum
fāma
lingua
locus
nauta
poēta
verbum

*A *declension* is a method of classifying nouns. There are five declensions in Latin.

**As you can see, these examples are in their nominative (subject) forms. Their genitive (possessive) singular forms would be puellae, agricolae, etc.

***Again, these examples are nominative forms. Their genitive singular forms would be amīcī, verbī, etc.

☐ Flashcards - (Add the new cards.)

Latin Workbook - Level 4
Copyright © 2000 by Karen Mohs

71

SECOND DECLENSION NEUTER NOUNS

Nouns of the second declension are usually masculine. However, sometimes they are neuter. Neuter second declension nouns end in -um.

Singular

Nominative	caelum	means	**the sky** (*subject of sentence*)
Genitive	caelī	means	**of the sky** (*shows possession*)
Dative	caelō	means	**to (or for) the sky** (*indirect object*)
Accusative	caelum	means	**the sky** (*direct object*)
Ablative	in caelō	means	**in the sky** (*ablative of place where*)

Plural

Nominative	caela	means	**the skies** (*subject of sentence*)
Genitive	caelōrum	means	**of the skies** (*shows possession*)
Dative	caelīs	means	**to (or for) the skies** (*indirect object*)
Accusative	caela	means	**the skies** (*direct object*)
Ablative	in caelīs	means	**in the skies** (*ablative of place where*)

(The singular "subject of sentence" and "direct object" endings are always the same in neuter nouns. The plural "subject of sentence" and "direct object" endings are always -a in neuter nouns.)

Circle the Latin words to match the English meanings.

of the skies	caelī	caelōrum	caela
with the word	verbōrum	verbīs	verbō
to the girls	puellārum	puellae	puellīs
for the woman	fēminae	fēminō	fēminīs
words	verbōs	verba	verbī
sons	filī	filiōs	filiīs
of the plain	campō	campōrum	campī
in the sky	in caelō	in caelīs	in caelā
waters	aquā	aquī	aquae

☐ Flashcards - (Add the new cards.)

72

Latin Workbook - Level 4
Copyright © 2000 by Karen Mohs

MORE SECOND DECLENSION NOUNS

We learned that nouns ending in -ī in the **genitive singular** belong to the second declension. To find the stem of a noun, remove the genitive singular **ending**.

Example: The genitive singular of amīcus is amīcī. Thus, the stem is amīc-.

Exception: Nouns ending in -ius are an exception to this rule. The genitive singular of fīlius is fīlī. However, the stem retains the -i- of fīlius even though the -i- is not in the genitive. Thus, the stem is fīli-.

Some words ending in -er are second declension nouns.

Singular

Nom.	puer	means **the boy**	ager	means	**the field**
Gen.	puerī	means **of the boy**	agrī	means	**of the field**
Dat.	puerō	means **to (or for) the boy**	agrō	means	**to (or for) the field**
Acc.	puerum	means **the boy**	agrum	means	**the field**
Abl.	cum puerō	means **with the boy**	in agrō	means	**in the field**

Plural

Nom.	puerī	means **the boys**	agrī	means	**the fields**
Gen.	puerōrum	means **of the boys**	agrōrum	means	**of the fields**
Dat.	puerīs	means **to (or for) the boys**	agrīs	means	**to (or for) the fields**
Acc.	puerōs	means **the boys**	agrōs	means	**the fields**
Abl.	cum puerīs	means **with the boys**	in agrīs	means	**in the fields**

Match the words to their genitive singular forms and to their stems.

carrus	agrī	agr-	puer	equī	puer-
populus	carrī	nūnti-	verbum	puerī	equa-
ager	populī	carr-	fīlius	verbī	amīciti-
nūntius	nūntī	agricol-	equus	fīlī	fīli-
dominus	agricolae	popul-	amīcitia	socī	verb-
agricola	dominī	domin-	socius	amīcitiae	soci-

☐ Flashcards - (Add the new cards.)

Latin Workbook - Level 4
Copyright © 2000 by Karen Mohs

73

LET'S PRACTICE

Circle the correct words.

sons	filī filiī filia	sky	caelum caelus caela
for the word	verbiō verbō verbōrum	for the sailor	nautīs nautō nautae
of the boys	puerōrum puerīs purō	territories	agerī agrī agera
for the swords	gladiīs gladīs gladiōs	of the grain	frūmentī frūmentum frūmentō
skies	caelōs caelī caela	allies	sociōs socia socōs
of the fields	agerōrum agrārum agrōrum	boys	puerae puerī puera
for the slaves	serviīs servīs servī	word	verba verbus verbum

☐ Flashcards

74

Latin Workbook - Level 4
Copyright © 2000 by Karen Mohs

Lesson 17

THIRD DECLENSION NOUNS

Just as nouns ending in -ae in the **genitive singular** belong to the *first declension* and those ending in -ī in the genitive singular belong to the *second declension*, now we learn that nouns ending in -is in the genitive singular belong to the *third declension*.

Singular

Nom.	frāter	means	**the brother** (*subject of sentence*)
Gen.	frātris	means	**of the brother** (*shows possession*)
Dat.	frātrī	means	**to (or for) the brother** (*indirect object*)
Acc.	frātrem	means	**the brother** (*direct object*)
Abl.	cum frātre	means	**with the brother** (*ablative of accompaniment*)

Plural

Nom.	frātrēs	means	**the brothers** (*subject of sentence*)
Gen.	frātrum	means	**of the brothers** (*shows possession*)
Dat.	frātribus	means	**to (or for) the brothers** (*indirect object*)
Acc.	frātrēs	means	**the brothers** (*direct object*)
Abl.	cum frātribus	means	**with the brothers** (*ablative of accompaniment*)

Let's try another one!

Singular

Nom.	soror	means	**the sister** (*subject of sentence*)
Gen.	sorōris	means	**of the sister** (*shows possession*)
Dat.	sorōrī	means	**to (or for) the sister** (*indirect object*)
Acc.	sorōrem	means	**the sister** (*direct object*)
Abl.	cum sorōre	means	**with the sister** (*ablative of accompaniment*)

Plural

Nom.	sorōrēs	means	**the sisters** (*subject of sentence*)
Gen.	sorōrum	means	**of the sisters** (*shows possession*)
Dat.	sorōribus	means	**to (or for) the sisters** (*indirect object*)
Acc.	sorōrēs	means	**the sisters** (*direct object*)
Abl.	cum sorōribus	means	**with the sisters** (*ablative of accompaniment*)

(Remember: To find the stem of a noun, remove the genitive singular ending.)

Circle the correctly spelled forms of frāter and soror.

sorōribus   frāterēs   sorōrōrum   frāteribus   sorōris   frātre

☐ Flashcards - (Add the new cards.)

Latin Workbook - Level 4
Copyright © 2000 by Karen Mohs

75

LET'S PRACTICE

Finish the words with the correct endings.

1. Frātr_____ means **of the brother**.

2. Verb_____ means **words**.

3. Puer_____ means **to the boy**.

4. Carr_____ means **for the wagons**.

5. Fīli_____ means **of the daughters**.

6. Fīli_____ means **of the sons**.

7. Frātr_____ means **to the brother**.

8. Sorōr_____ means **for the sisters**.

9. Cael_____ means **sky**.

10. Frūment_____ means **for the grain**.

11. Frātr_____ means **of the brothers**.

12. Sorōr_____ means **sisters**.

13. Tub_____ means **on the trumpets**.

14. Agr_____ means **of the territory**.

15. Puer_____ means **for the boys**.

☐ Flashcards

76

Latin Workbook - Level 4
Copyright © 2000 by Karen Mohs

LET'S PRACTICE

Put the correct endings on these Latin words.

ēs ō is em	1. I see the brother and the sisters of the king. Frātr_____ et sorōr_____ rēg_____ vide_____.	
a am ī ō	2. The woman in the field praises the language of the ally. Fēmin_____ in agr_____ lingu_____ soc_____ laudat.	
ne am ae a	3. Are you the wife of the sailor? Es_____ fēmin_____ naut_____?	
ī a ō ā	4. With boldness, I write the words to the mother. Cum audāci_____ mātr_____ verb_____ scrīb_____.	
a ōs ant ārum	5. They look at the skies and the fields of the provinces. Cael_____ et agr_____ prōvinci_____ spect_____.	
at a am īs	6. The poet declares with words the boldness of the tribes. Poēt_____ audāci_____ populī verb_____ cōnfīrm_____.	
am āmus ā ō	7. Meanwhile, we carry the water to the boy in the farmhouse. Interim puer_____ aqu_____ in vīll_____ port_____.	
ōs ā ēx at	8. The king calls together the messengers with a trumpet. R_____ nūnti_____ tub_____ convoc_____.	
at ā a ant	9. The girl often walks in the forest for a long time. Puell_____ saepe in silv_____ diū ambul_____.	
am is ās que	10. You love the native land of the sister and of the brother. Patri_____ sorōr_____ frātris_____ am_____.	

☐ Flashcards

Latin Workbook - Level 4
Copyright © 2000 by Karen Mohs

77

LET'S PRACTICE

Write the meanings beside the Latin words.

māter _____   mātrēs _____

mātris _____   mātrum _____

mātrī _____   mātribus _____

mātrem _____   mātrēs _____

cum mātre _____   cum mātribus _____

---

rēx _____   rēgēs _____

rēgis _____   rēgum _____

rēgī _____   rēgibus _____

rēgem _____   rēgēs _____

cum rēge _____   cum rēgibus _____

---

verbum _____   verba _____

verbī _____   verbōrum _____

verbō _____   verbīs _____

verbum _____   verba _____

verbō _____   verbīs _____

☐ Flashcards

Lesson 18

THIRD DECLENSION "I-STEM" NOUNS

As we have learned, most third declension nouns end with -um in the **genitive plural**. However, there is a group of third declension nouns that end in -ium in the genitive plural. These special nouns are called "third declension i-stems."

"I-STEM" CLUE #1

Does the masculine or feminine noun end with -ēs or -is? Does it have the same number of syllables in both the **nominative** (subject) and **genitive** (possessive) cases? Yes? Then the noun is an "i-stem."

Singular

Nom.	hostis	means	**the enemy** (*subject of sentence*)
Gen.	hostis	means	**of the enemy** (*shows possession*)
Dat.	hostī	means	**to (or for) the enemy** (*indirect object*)
Acc.	hostem	means	**the enemy** (*direct object*)
Abl.	cum hoste	means	**with the enemy** (*ablative of accompaniment*)

Plural

Nom.	hostēs	means	**the enemies** (*subject of sentence*)
Gen.	hostium	means	**of the enemies** (*shows possession*)
Dat.	hostibus	means	**to (or for) the enemies** (*indirect object*)
Acc.	hostēs	means	**the enemies** (*direct object*)
Abl.	cum hostibus	means	**with the enemies** (*ablative of accompaniment*)

Circle the correct words.

of the enemies	enemies	for the enemy
hostium hostī	hostēs hostis	hostium hostī
enemy	with the enemy	of the enemy
hostī hostibus hostem	cum hostium cum hostis cum hoste	hostis hostēs hostibus

☐ Flashcards - (Add the new cards.)

Latin Workbook - Level 4
Copyright © 2000 by Karen Mohs

79

MORE THIRD DECLENSION "I-STEM" NOUNS

"I-STEM" CLUE #2

Does the masculine or feminine noun end with **-ns** or **-rs**? Yes? Then the noun is an "i-stem."

Singular

Nom.	gēns	means	**the nation** (*subject of sentence*)
Gen.	gentis	means	**of the nation** (*shows possession*)
Dat.	gentī	means	**to (or for) the nation** (*indirect object*)
Acc.	gentem	means	**the nation** (*direct object*)
Abl.	cum gente	means	**with the nation** (*ablative of accompaniment*)

Plural

Nom.	gentēs	means	**the nations** (*subject of sentence*)
Gen.	gentium	means	**of the nations** (*shows possession*)
Dat.	gentibus	means	**to (or for) the nations** (*indirect object*)
Acc.	gentēs	means	**the nations** (*direct object*)
Abl.	cum gentibus	means	**with the nations** (*ablative of accompaniment*)

"I-STEM" CLUE #3

Is the masculine or feminine noun only one syllable? And does the stem* end in two consonants? Yes? Then the noun is an "i-stem."

Singular

Nom.	urbs	means	**the city** (*subject of sentence*)
Gen.	urbis	means	**of the city** (*shows possession*)
Dat.	urbī	means	**to (or for) the city** (*indirect object*)
Acc.	urbem	means	**the city** (*direct object*)
Abl.	in urbe	means	**in the city** (*ablative of place where*)

Plural

Nom.	urbēs	means	**the cities** (*subject of sentence*)
Gen.	urbium	means	**of the cities** (*shows possession*)
Dat.	urbibus	means	**to (or for) the cities** (*indirect object*)
Acc.	urbēs	means	**the cities** (*direct object*)
Abl.	in urbibus	means	**in the cities** (*ablative of place where*)

*Remember: To find the stem of a noun, remove the genitive singular ending.

☐ Flashcards - (Add the new cards.)

MORE THIRD DECLENSION "I-STEM" NOUNS

"I-STEM" CLUE #4

Does the **neuter** noun end with -al or -e? Yes? Then the noun is an "i-stem." Notice that these neuter "i-stems" have -ī instead of -e in the ablative singular form and -ia instead of -ēs in the nominative and accusative plural forms.

Singular

Nom.	mare	means	**the sea** (*subject of sentence*)
Gen.	maris	means	**of the sea** (*shows possession*)
Dat.	marī	means	**to (or for) the sea** (*indirect object*)
Acc.	mare	means	**the sea** (*direct object*)
Abl.	in marī	means	**in the sea** (*ablative of place where*)

Plural

Nom.	maria	means	**the seas** (*subject of sentence*)
Gen.	marium	means	**of the seas** (*shows possession*)
Dat.	maribus	means	**to (or for) the seas** (*indirect object*)
Acc.	maria	means	**the seas** (*direct object*)
Abl.	in maribus	means	**in the seas** (*ablative of place where*)

Write the third declension nouns on the right under the correct headings.

"i-stem"	not "i-stem"
_____	_____
_____	_____
_____	_____
_____	_____
_____	_____
_____	_____
_____	_____
_____	_____
_____	_____

frāter
gēns
hostis
mare
māter
mors
rēx
soror
urbs

☐ Flashcards - (Add the new cards.)

Latin Workbook - Level 4
Copyright © 2000 by Karen Mohs

81

LET'S PRACTICE

Write the meanings beside the Latin words.

mors _____   mortēs _____

mortis _____   mortium _____

mortī _____   mortibus _____

mortem _____   mortēs _____

morte _____   mortibus _____

---

mare _____   maria _____

maris _____   marium _____

marī _____   maribus _____

mare _____   maria _____

in marī _____   in maribus _____

---

vir _____   virī _____

virī _____   virōrum _____

virō _____   virīs _____

virum _____   virōs _____

cum virō _____   cum virīs _____

☐ Flashcards

82

Latin Workbook - Level 4
Copyright © 2000 by Karen Mohs

Lesson 19

LATIN VERBS - CONJUGATION

Latin verbs are grouped according to their *conjugation*.

First conjugation:
The present stem* of these verbs ends in -ā-.

Examples: vocō vocāre vocāvī vocātum
laudō laudāre laudāvī laudātum

Second conjugation:
The present stem of these verbs ends in -ē-.

Examples: sedeō sedēre sēdī sessum
maneō manēre mānsī mānsum

(We will learn about **third**, "**third i-stem**," and **fourth** conjugations later.)

SECOND CONJUGATION VERBS

sedeō means **I sit.**   sedēmus means **We sit.**

sedēs means **You** (singular) **sit.**   sedētis means **You** (plural) **sit.**

sedet means **He (she, it) sits.**   sedent means **They sit.**

Match the words to their meanings.

manēs   they answer

sedēmus   you stay

respondent   we sit

videō   he remains

respondētis   you reply

manet   I see

*Remember: To find the present stem of most verbs, remove the -re from the **second** principal part. See page 39.

☐ Flashcards - (Add the new cards.)

Latin Workbook - Level 4
Copyright © 2000 by Karen Mohs

83

LET'S PRACTICE

Write the correct Latin words in these sentences.

1. _____

   It means **We guard the brothers.**

2. _____

   It means **They remain in the city.**

3. _____

   It means **She sits on the horse.**

4. _____

   It means **I often choose the grain.**

5. _____

   It means **You answer with boldness.**

6. _____

   It means **Are they the enemy?***

7. _____

   It means **You love the mother and the sister.**

8. _____

   It means **We see the earth and the seas.**

amās
cum audāciā
dēligō
frātrēs
frūmentum
hostēs
in equō
in urbe
manent
mariaque
mātrem
respondētis
saepe
sedet
servāmus
sorōremque
suntne
terram
vidēmus

*The word hostis means "a public enemy" or "an enemy of the state." More than one of these enemies may be translated into English as "the enemy." However, in Latin, the plural should be used.

☐ Flashcards

84

Latin Workbook - Level 4
Copyright © 2000 by Karen Mohs

LET'S PRACTICE

Circle the correct conjugations for these verbs.

occupō	first	second	sedent	first	second
videō	first	second	oppugnō	first	second
parant	first	second	manet	first	second
nāvigātis	first	second	temptant	first	second
servat	first	second	respondeō	first	second
vocās	first	second	vidēmus	first	second
pugnō	first	second	līberās	first	second
ambulant	first	second	portō	first	second
labōrātis	first	second	maneō	first	second
sedeō	first	second	superās	first	second
respondent	first	second	dēmōnstrō	first	second
clāmāmus	first	second	nārrātis	first	second
servō	first	second	volō	first	second
manēs	first	second	vidēs	first	second
spectat	first	second	exspectant	first	second
appellō	first	second	nūntiō	first	second
convocat	first	second	habitat	first	second
sedētis	first	second	cōnfirmās	first	second
dēlectō	first	second	laudō	first	second
amō	first	second	vident	first	second

☐ Flashcards

Latin Workbook - Level 4
Copyright © 2000 by Karen Mohs

85

LET'S PRACTICE

Write the meanings of the Latin words. On the last set, write the Latin words.

videō _____

vidēs _____

videt _____

portō _____

portās _____

portat _____

maneō _____

manēs _____

manet _____

pugnō _____

pugnās _____

pugnat _____

sedeō _____

sedēs _____

sedet _____

līberō _____

līberās _____

līberat _____

I reply _____

you (sing.) reply _____

he (she, it) replies _____

vidēmus _____

vidētis _____

vident _____

portāmus _____

portātis _____

portant _____

manēmus _____

manētis _____

manent _____

pugnāmus _____

pugnātis _____

pugnant _____

sedēmus _____

sedētis _____

sedent _____

līberāmus _____

līberātis _____

līberant _____

we reply _____

you (pl.) reply _____

they reply _____

☐ Flashcards

86

Latin Workbook - Level 4
Copyright © 2000 by Karen Mohs

Lesson 20

THIRD CONJUGATION VERBS

Just as verbs whose second principal part ends in -āre are first conjugation verbs and verbs whose second principal part ends in -ēre are second conjugation verbs, now we learn that verbs whose second principal part ends in -ere (no macron) are **third conjugation** verbs.

The **present stem** of a third conjugation verb is found in a special way. Unlike first and second conjugation verbs, whose present stems are found by dropping the -re from the **second** principal part, the present stem of a third conjugation verb is found by dropping the -ō from the **first** principal part.

Example: dīcō dīcere dīxī dictum
The present stem is dīc-.

dīcō means **I say.**   dīcimus means **We say.**

dīcis means **You** (singular) **say.**   dīcitis means **You** (plural) **say.**

dīcit means **He** (**she**, **it**) **says.**   dīcunt means **They say.**

(Notice the -i- or the -u- inserted between the present tense stem
and the ending in all but the first word.)

Match the words to their meanings.

dīcit   she tells

dēligō   you bring

dūcitis   I choose

dēligunt   we write

scrībimus   you lead

dūcis   they choose

☐ Flashcards - (Add the new cards.)

Latin Workbook - Level 4
Copyright © 2000 by Karen Mohs

87

LET'S PRACTICE

Circle the correct conjugations for these verbs.

scrībis	first	second	third	temptō	first	second	third
manēmus	first	second	third	scrībitis	first	second	third
nāvigās	first	second	third	videō	first	second	third
sedēs	first	second	third	dīcis	first	second	third
dīcunt	first	second	third	dēligimus	first	second	third
dūcimus	first	second	third	manētis	first	second	third
cōnfirmant	first	second	third	respondeō	first	second	third
videt	first	second	third	līberat	first	second	third
dēligitis	first	second	third	scrībō	first	second	third
occupās	first	second	third	dīcit	first	second	third
scrībunt	first	second	third	volātis	first	second	third
sedēmus	first	second	third	manent	first	second	third
manet	first	second	third	dūcit	first	second	third
vocāmus	first	second	third	respondēs	first	second	third
dīcō	first	second	third	vidētis	first	second	third
dēligō	first	second	third	dūcō	first	second	third
dūcis	first	second	third	pugnāmus	first	second	third
parat	first	second	third	respondet	first	second	third
vident	first	second	third	dēligit	first	second	third
sedet	first	second	third	laudō	first	second	third

☐ Flashcards

LET'S PRACTICE

Circle the correct words.

1. The word **videō** is the (first, second, third, fourth) principal part of the (first, second, third) conjugation verb **videō**.

2. The word **scrībere** is the (first, second, third, fourth) principal part of the (first, second, third) conjugation verb **scrībō**.

3. The word **vocātum** is the (first, second, third, fourth) principal part of the (first, second, third) conjugation verb **vocō**.

4. The word **respondī** is the (first, second, third, fourth) principal part of the (first, second, third) conjugation verb **respondeō**.

5. The word **amāvī** is the (first, second, third, fourth) principal part of the (first, second, third) conjugation verb **amō**.

6. The word **dīxī** is the (first, second, third, fourth) principal part of the (first, second, third) conjugation verb **dīcō**.

7. The word **mānsum** is the (first, second, third, fourth) principal part of the (first, second, third) conjugation verb **maneō**.

8. The word **sedēre** is the (first, second, third, fourth) principal part of the (first, second, third) conjugation verb **sedeō**.

9. The word **dēlēctum** is the (first, second, third, fourth) principal part of the (first, second, third) conjugation verb **dēligō**.

10. The word **appellāre** is the (first, second, third, fourth) principal part of the (first, second, third) conjugation verb **appellō**.

☐ Flashcards

Latin Workbook - Level 4
Copyright © 2000 by Karen Mohs

89

LET'S PRACTICE

Write the meanings of the Latin words. On the last set, write the Latin words.

dūcō _____

dūcis _____

dūcit _____

dūcimus _____

dūcitis _____

dūcunt _____

respondeō _____

respondēs _____

respondet _____

respondēmus _____

respondētis _____

respondent _____

vulnerō _____

vulnerās _____

vulnerat _____

vulnerāmus _____

vulnerātis _____

vulnerant _____

scrībō _____

scrībis _____

scrībit _____

scrībimus _____

scrībitis _____

scrībunt _____

maneō _____

manēs _____

manet _____

manēmus _____

manētis _____

manent _____

dēlectō _____

dēlectās _____

dēlectat _____

dēlectāmus _____

dēlectātis _____

dēlectant _____

I choose _____

you (sing.) choose _____

he (she, it) chooses _____

we choose _____

you (pl.) choose _____

they choose _____

☐ Flashcards

90

Latin Workbook - Level 4
Copyright © 2000 by Karen Mohs

Lesson 21

nōmen
nōminis (neuter)

means

name

Write the Latin word that means **name**.

Write the Latin word that means **I make**.

faciō
facere fēcī factum

means

I make, I do

veniō
venīre vēnī ventum

means

I come

Write the Latin word that means **I come**.

☐ Flashcards - (Add the new cards.)

Latin Workbook - Level 4
Copyright © 2000 by Karen Mohs

91

LET'S PRACTICE

Write the meanings of the following Latin words.

videō _____

mare _____

hostis _____

verbum _____

faciō _____

scrībō _____

interim _____

vir _____

nōmen _____

gēns _____

maneō _____

caelum _____

respondeō _____

veniō _____

dūcō _____

māter _____

rēx _____

urbs _____

sedeō _____

frāter _____

mors _____

dīcō _____

soror _____

frūmentum _____

dēligō _____

☐ Flashcards

manus
manūs (feminine)
means
hand, band (of men)

Write the Latin word that means **hand**.

Write the Latin word that means **I listen to**.

audiō
audīre audīvī audītum
means
I hear, I listen to

diēs
diēī (masculine and feminine)
means
day

Write the Latin word that means **day**.

☐ Flashcards - (Add the new cards.)

Latin Workbook - Level 4
Copyright © 2000 by Karen Mohs

93

LET'S PRACTICE

Match the words to their meanings.

mors	death
mare	name
nōmen	sea
frāter	brother
faciō	I make, I do
frūmentum	grain
dīcō	day
diēs	I lead, I bring
dūcō	I say, I tell
hostis	I sit
soror	sister
sedeō	enemy
manus	mother
maneō	hand, band (of men)
māter	I stay, I remain
veniō	I hear, I listen to
audiō	I come
dēligō	I choose
urbs	nation, family, clan
respondeō	I answer, I reply
gēns	city

☐ Flashcards

94

Latin Workbook - Level 4
Copyright © 2000 by Karen Mohs

Lesson 22

capiō

capere cēpī captum

means

I take, I capture

Write the Latin word that means **I take**.

Write the Latin word that means **I know**.

sciō

scīre scīvī scītum

means

I know

iter

itineris (neuter)

means

route, journey, march

Write the Latin word that means **journey**.

☐ Flashcards - (Add the new cards.)

Latin Workbook - Level 4
Copyright © 2000 by Karen Mohs

95

LET'S PRACTICE

Match the Latin words to their meanings.

_____	1. maneō	a.	I bring
_____	2. veniō	b.	I tell
_____	3. dūcō	c.	I remain
_____	4. sedeō	d.	I listen to
_____	5. faciō	e.	I do
_____	6. capiō	f.	I know
_____	7. sciō	g.	I answer
_____	8. dīcō	h.	I come
_____	9. dēligō	i.	I choose
_____	10. respondeō	j.	I take
_____	11. audiō	k.	I sit
_____	12. frūmentum	l.	day
_____	13. manus	m.	mother
_____	14. diēs	n.	city
_____	15. hostis	o.	sister
_____	16. iter	p.	name
_____	17. urbs	q.	death
_____	18. soror	r.	grain
_____	19. māter	s.	sea
_____	20. gēns	t.	brother
_____	21. nōmen	u.	enemy
_____	22. mors	v.	journey
_____	23. frāter	w.	clan
_____	24. mare	x.	band (of men)

☐ Flashcards

96

Latin Workbook - Level 4
Copyright © 2000 by Karen Mohs

invenio
invenīre invēnī inventum
means
I come upon, I find

Write the Latin word that means **I come upon**.

Write the Latin word that means **faith**.

fidēs
fideī (feminine)

means

faith, loyalty, pledge, confidence

pater
patris (masculine)

means

father

(if plural: **senators**)

Write the Latin word that means **father**.

☐ Flashcards - (Add the new cards.)

Latin Workbook - Level 4
Copyright © 2000 by Karen Mohs

97

LET'S PRACTICE

Circle the correct words.

name	I sit	enemy
nōmen verbum nunc	soror sedeō stō	hostis vir inopia
death	day	hand
caelum mors male	diū annus diēs	gēns hōra manus
father	I remain	I make
rēx pater vīlla	maneō occupō labōrō	mare servō faciō
mother	I hear	march
māter fēmina cōpia	audiō dīcō vocō	iter urbs fāma
I come upon	I come	I choose
spectō inveniō parō	videō portō veniō	dēligō dūcō respondeō
I know	I capture	faith
scrībō superō sciō	vulnerō pugnō capiō	frāter fidēs frūmentum

☐ Flashcards

98

Latin Workbook - Level 4
Copyright © 2000 by Karen Mohs

Lesson 23

accipiō
accipere accēpī acceptum
means
I receive, I accept

Write the Latin word that means **I receive**.

Write the Latin word that means **man**.

homō
hominis (masculine or feminine)
means
human being, man

cōnsilium
cōnsilī (neuter)
means
plan, advice,
foresight

Write the Latin word that means **plan**.

☐ Flashcards - (Add the new cards.)

Latin Workbook - Level 4
Copyright © 2000 by Karen Mohs

99

LET'S PRACTICE

Circle the correct words.

route	caelum iter nōmen	I listen to	dīcō videō audiō
I come	maneō veniō clāmō	I take	capiō dūcō convocō
loyalty	fidēs frāter māter	I find	laudō inveniō sedeō
I know	dēligō cōnfirmō sciō	I do	dēmōnstrō dō faciō
plan	mare cōnsilium verbum	senators	patrēs sorōrēs virī
band (of men)	manus gēns hostis	day	urbs mors diēs
I receive	respondeō scrībō accipiō	human being	rēx homō frūmentum

☐ Flashcards

100

Latin Workbook - Level 4
Copyright © 2000 by Karen Mohs

reperiō
reperīre repperī repertum
means
I find, I discover

Write the Latin word that means **I discover**.

Write the Latin word that means **hope**.

spēs
speī (feminine)
means
hope

vēritās
vēritātis (feminine)
means
truth, trueness

Write the Latin word that means **truth**.

☐ Flashcards - (Add the new cards.)

Latin Workbook - Level 4
Copyright © 2000 by Karen Mohs

101

LET'S PRACTICE

Write the meanings of the following Latin words.

diēs _____

reperiō _____

veniō _____

sciō _____

dēligō _____

pater _____

faciō _____

inveniō _____

soror _____

capiō _____

manus _____

vēritās _____

homō _____

māter _____

cōnsilium _____

sedeō _____

iter _____

hostis _____

audiō _____

mors _____

nōmen _____

accipiō _____

spēs _____

maneō _____

fidēs _____

☐ Flashcards

102

Latin Workbook - Level 4
Copyright © 2000 by Karen Mohs

Lesson 24

senātus

senātūs (masculine)

means

senate

Write the Latin word that means **senate**.

Write the Latin word that means **crowd**.

multitūdō

multitūdinis (feminine)

means

great number, crowd

ecce

means

behold

Write the Latin word that means **behold**.

☐ Flashcards - (Add the new cards.)

Latin Workbook - Level 4
Copyright © 2000 by Karen Mohs

103

LET'S PRACTICE

Circle the Latin words to match the English meanings.

I discover	videō	reperiō	respondeō
I come	veniō	dō	cōnfirmō
I hear	clāmō	habitō	audiō
truth	vēritās	caelum	audācia
father	māter	pater	frāter
I know	nārrō	sciō	dēlectō
behold	ecce	hostis	cūr
foresight	mare	cōnsilium	causa
great number	frūmentum	locus	multitūdō
I find	maneō	inveniō	līberō
man	homō	gēns	iam
hope	vir	mors	spēs
I capture	dūcō	capiō	scrībō
route	iter	lūdus	ager
senate	senātus	epistula	carrus
day	rēx	hodiē	diēs
I accept	sedeō	dīcō	accipiō
pledge	dēligō	fidēs	soror
hand	manus	dominus	fortūna
name	urbs	nōmen	verbum
I make	labōrō	convocō	faciō

☐ Flashcards

104

Latin Workbook - Level 4
Copyright © 2000 by Karen Mohs

LET'S PRACTICE

Write the correct Latin verbs, including all four principal parts.

I take

I stay

I say

I come

I sit

I come
upon

I see

I love

I lead

I discover

I hear

I write

I do

I know

I choose

I receive

☐ Flashcards

Latin Workbook - Level 4
Copyright © 2000 by Karen Mohs

105

LET'S PRACTICE

Match the nouns to their genitive singular forms and to their meanings.

caelum	caelī	human being
spēs	hominis	sky
homō	speī	hope
mare	fideī	confidence
multitūdō	maris	sea
fidēs	multitūdinis	great number
frāter	frūmentī	brother
frūmentum	frātris	father
pater	patris	grain
nōmen	nōminis	death
mors	mortis	name
urbs	urbis	city
manus	vēritātis	journey
iter	itineris	hand
vēritās	manūs	truth
soror	diēī	senate
senātus	sorōris	sister
diēs	senātūs	day
gēns	cōnsilī	advice
hostis	gentis	enemy
cōnsilium	hostis	family

☐ Flashcards

106

Latin Workbook - Level 4
Copyright © 2000 by Karen Mohs

LET'S PRACTICE

Write these sentences in Latin.

1. Behold, today we see the sailor's cart.

2. The fathers sit in the city of the poet's sons.

3. You (sing.) say a word to the sister of the queen's husband.

4. The kings' families stay in the fields for a long time.

5. Why do you (pl.) choose the grain and horses?

6. The band (of men) sees the poverty of the crowds.

7. We love the city of the king and queen.

☐ Flashcards

PUZZLE TIME!

Unscramble the following Latin words. Put them in the sentences below.
Write what the sentences mean.

tse _____

ēhosst _____

bciīrst _____

hiimnos _____

agonnpptu _____

āeēimrttv _____

1. _____ rēgem gladiō semper _____.

   It means _____

2. Puer _____ mortem equī nōn amat.

   It means _____

3. Agricolae _____ vident, sed verbum nōn scrībunt.

   It means _____

4. Soror fābulam _____, et frāter hostem superat.

   It means _____

5. Spēs hominis _____ vēritās et vīta.

   It means _____

☐ Flashcards

108

Latin Workbook - Level 4
Copyright © 2000 by Karen Mohs

Lesson 25

THIRD DECLENSION NEUTER NOUNS

Singular
Nom.   **nōmen** means **the name** (*subject of sentence*)
Gen.   **nōminis** means **of the name** (*shows possession*)
Dat.   **nōminī** means **to (or for) the name** (*indirect object*)
Acc.   **nōmen** means **the name** (*direct object*)
Abl.   **nōmine** means **with the name** (*ablative of means*)

Plural
Nom.   **nōmina** means **the names** (*subject of sentence*)
Gen.   **nōminum** means **of the names** (*shows possession*)
Dat.   **nōminibus** means **to (or for) the names** (*indirect object*)
Acc.   **nōmina** means **the names** (*direct object*)
Abl.   **nōminibus** means **with the names** (*ablative of means*)

(The singular "subject of sentence" and "direct object" endings are always the same in neuter nouns.
The plural "subject of sentence" and "direct object" endings are always -a.)

Circle the correct words.

of the name	for the names	for the marches
nōminis nōmen nōminibus	nōminis nōminibus nōmen	itineribus iter itinera
names	of the names	of the journeys
nōmina nōmine nōminum	nōminum nōminis nōmina	itinere itinera itinerum
for the journey	of the route	to the name
itineribus itinerī iter	itineribus itinera itineris	nōminibus nōminī nōmen

☐ Flashcards - (Add the new cards.)

Latin Workbook - Level 4
Copyright © 2000 by Karen Mohs

109

LET'S PRACTICE

Write the Latin words to complete the sentences. Write their meanings.

1. Nōmina _____ hostium nunc sciō.
   (of the cities)

   It means _____

2. Cūr cōnsilium captivōrum _____?
   (I accept)

   It means _____

3. Multitūdinēs īnsulārum in _____ reperiō.
   (the sea)

   It means _____

4. Patrēs frātrēsque in urbibus _____ saepe manent.
   (of the kings)

   It means _____

5. Iter* in _____ et in terrā rēginae faciō.
   (the province)

   It means _____

6. Veniō, sed cum audāciā _____ nōn dīcō.
   (the truth)

   It means _____

7. Lēgātī soror gentem _____ et aquam servat.
   (leads)

   It means _____

*The words iter and faciō together mean "march."

☐ Flashcards

110

Latin Workbook - Level 4
Copyright © 2000 by Karen Mohs

LET'S PRACTICE

Circle the Latin words to match the English meanings.

seas	maribus	maria	marium
you choose	dēligunt	dēligimus	dēligis
for the sister	sorōrī	sorōrēs	sorōribus
foresight	cōnsilī	cōnsilia	cōnsilium
of the enemies	hostibus	hostium	hostis
senators	patrēs	pater	patribus
for the deaths	mortibus	mortī	mortium
they bring	dūcimus	dūcit	dūcunt
brothers	frātrī	frātrēs	frātrum
of the truths	vēritātum	vēritās	vēritātis
for man	hominī	homō	hominum
with the grain	frūmentī	frūmentōrum	frūmentō
we sit	sedēs	sedēmus	sedent
of the cities	urbis	urbium	urbs
you tell	dīcimus	dīcis	dīcunt
crowd	multitūdinis	multitūdinēs	multitūdō
for the clan	gentī	gentis	gentibus
of the name	nōminis	nōmen	nōminibus
you remain	maneō	manētis	manet
for the mothers	mātribus	mātrēs	māter
she replies	respondētis	respondent	respondet

☐ Flashcards

Latin Workbook - Level 4
Copyright © 2000 by Karen Mohs

111

LET'S PRACTICE

Write the meanings beside the Latin words.

vēritās _____   vēritātēs _____

vēritātis _____   vēritātum _____

vēritātī _____   vēritātibus _____

vēritātem _____   vēritātēs _____

vēritāte _____   vēritātibus _____

iter _____   itinera _____

itineris _____   itinerum _____

itinerī _____   itineribus _____

iter _____   itinera _____

itinere _____   itineribus _____

hostis _____   hostēs _____

hostis _____   hostium _____

hostī _____   hostibus _____

hostem _____   hostēs _____

cum hoste _____   cum hostibus _____

☐ Flashcards

112

Latin Workbook - Level 4
Copyright © 2000 by Karen Mohs

Lesson 26

QUESTIONS (YES & NO)

EXPECTS EITHER *YES* OR *NO* ANSWER

As we have learned, to make a sentence into a question which has a *yes* or *no* answer, we simply add -ne to the end of the first word in the sentence.

Puellam laudat.   It means **He praises the girl.**
Puellamne laudat?   It means **Does he praise the girl?**

The answer?

Yes, he praises the girl. or No, he does not praise the girl.

EXPECTS *YES* ANSWER

What if you *expect* a *yes* answer? Use a negative word (usually nōn) with the -ne attached to it at the beginning of the sentence.

Nōnne puellam laudat?   It means **He praises the girl, doesn't he?**

The answer?

Yes, he praises the girl.

EXPECTS *NO* ANSWER

What if you *expect* a *no* answer? Use the word num at the beginning of the sentence.

Num puellam laudat?   It means **He doesn't praise the girl, does he?**

The answer?

No, he does not praise the girl.

☐ Flashcards - (Add the new cards.)

Latin Workbook - Level 4
Copyright © 2000 by Karen Mohs

LET'S PRACTICE

Circle **yes** if the question expects a *yes* answer. Circle **no** if it expects a *no* answer. Circle **either** if it can be answered with either *yes* or *no*. Circle **neither** if it cannot be answered with *yes* or *no*. Write the meanings.

1. Cūr vir tubam dēligit?   yes   no   either   neither

   It means _____

2. Num lēgātus gladium portat?   yes   no   either   neither

   It means _____

3. Nōnne nautae īnsulās vident?   yes   no   either   neither

   It means _____

4. Agricolaene epistulās scrībunt? yes   no   either   neither

   It means _____

_____

Write nōnne or num to introduce the questions.

1. _____ frūmentum equōsque dēligis?

   It means **You choose the grain and the horses, don't you?**

2. _____ servī in urbe manent?

   It means **The slaves don't stay in the city, do they?**

3. _____ soror frātrem dūcit?

   It means **The sister doesn't lead the brother, does she?**

4. _____ in agrō sedētis et vīllās spectātis?

   It means **You sit in the field and look at the farmhouses, don't you?**

☐ Flashcards

114

Latin Workbook - Level 4
Copyright © 2000 by Karen Mohs

LET'S PRACTICE

Match the letters of the questions to the correct answers below.

a. Nōnne gentēs vēritātem verbōrum dominī dīcunt?

b. Num hodiē in īnsulā iter faciō?

c. Gentēsne vēritātem verbōrum dominī dīcunt?

d. Fēminane rēgī pecūniam portat?

e. Nōnne hodiē in īnsulā iter faciō?

f. Hodiēne in īnsulā iter faciō?

g. Cūr fēmina rēgī pecūniam portat?

h. Num fēmina rēgī pecūniam portat?

i. Nōnne fēmina rēgī pecūniam portat?

j. Num gentēs vēritātem verbōrum dominī dīcunt?

( ) 1. The woman serves the king by carrying his money.

( ) 2. No, the woman doesn't carry the money to the king.

( ) 3. No, you don't march on the island today.

( ) 4. Yes, the clans tell the truth of the master's words.

( ) 5. Yes, the woman carries the money to the king.

( ) 6. You may or may not march on the island today.

( ) 7. The woman may or may not carry the money to the king.

( ) 8. No, the clans don't tell the truth of the master's words.

( ) 9. The clans may or may not tell the truth of the master's words.

( ) 10. Yes, you march on the island today.

☐ Flashcards

Latin Workbook - Level 4
Copyright © 2000 by Karen Mohs

115

LET'S PRACTICE

Answer the following Latin questions with complete Latin sentences.*
Write the meanings of the questions.

1. Suntne equī cum virīs in prōvinciā?

   _____

   _____

   The question means _____

2. Nōnne frāter sorōrēsque sunt amīcī?

   _____

   _____

   The question means _____

3. Num in silvā hodiē ambulās?

   _____

   _____

   The question means _____

4. Nōnne rēgem rēginamque vidētis?

   _____

   _____

   The question means _____

5. Num multitūdinibus epistulam scrībis?

   _____

   _____

   The question means _____

6. Num in marī nunc habitātis?

   _____

   _____

   The question means _____

7. Servōsne in patriā semper līberās?

   _____

   _____

   The question means _____

*Complete sentences are used here to provide practice in Latin sentence structure. In a future workbook in this series, we will learn the Latin way to answer Latin questions.

☐ Flashcards

116

Latin Workbook - Level 4
Copyright © 2000 by Karen Mohs

LET'S PRACTICE

Circle the correct genders (**m** for *masculine*, **f** for *feminine*, **n** for *neuter*).
Circle the correct declensions (**1st** for *first declension*, **2nd** for *second declension*, **3rd** for *third declension*, and **3rd-I** for *third declension i-stem*).

amīcus	m	f	n	1st	2nd	3rd	3rd-I
caelum	m	f	n	1st	2nd	3rd	3rd-I
gēns	m	f	n	1st	2nd	3rd	3rd-I
frūmentum	m	f	n	1st	2nd	3rd	3rd-I
rēx	m	f	n	1st	2nd	3rd	3rd-I
agricola	m	f	n	1st	2nd	3rd	3rd-I
mors	m	f	n	1st	2nd	3rd	3rd-I
pater	m	f	n	1st	2nd	3rd	3rd-I
vir	m	f	n	1st	2nd	3rd	3rd-I
urbs	m	f	n	1st	2nd	3rd	3rd-I
puella	m	f	n	1st	2nd	3rd	3rd-I
multitūdō	m	f	n	1st	2nd	3rd	3rd-I
iter	m	f	n	1st	2nd	3rd	3rd-I
mare	m	f	n	1st	2nd	3rd	3rd-I
vēritās	m	f	n	1st	2nd	3rd	3rd-I
hostis	m	f	n	1st	2nd	3rd	3rd-I
cōnsilium	m	f	n	1st	2nd	3rd	3rd-I
māter	m	f	n	1st	2nd	3rd	3rd-I
socius	m	f	n	1st	2nd	3rd	3rd-I
nōmen	m	f	n	1st	2nd	3rd	3rd-I

☐ Flashcards

Latin Workbook - Level 4
Copyright © 2000 by Karen Mohs

LET'S PRACTICE

Write the words on the right under the correct headings.

first declension

second declension

third declension

third declension i-stem

annus
causa
cōnsilium
dīligentia
frāter
frūmentum
fuga
gēns
homō
hostis
mare
māter
mors
nātūra
nōmen
pater
poena
poēta
puer
soror
urbs
verbum
vir

☐ Flashcards

Lesson 27

THIRD CONJUGATION "I-STEM" VERBS

We have learned three conjugations of Latin verbs:

Ending of Second Principal Part	Conjugation
-āre	first
-ēre	second
-ere	third

Now we will learn a variation of the third conjugation, called the ***third conjugation i-stem***. I-stems have the -ere ending on the second principal part, just like other third conjugation verbs. The difference is in the stem (found by removing the -ō from the first principal part). This new stem ends with an -i-.

Example: capiō capere cēpī captum
The present stem is capi-.

capiō means **I take.**   capimus means **We take.**

capis means **You** (singular) **take.**   capitis means **You** (plural) **take.**

capit means **He** (**she**, **it**) **takes.**   capiunt means **They take.**

Match the words to their meanings.

capimus   you accept

accipitis   he receives

accipit   we take

faciō   they do

faciunt   I make

capis   you capture

☐ Flashcards - (Add the new cards.)

Latin Workbook - Level 4
Copyright © 2000 by Karen Mohs

119

LET'S PRACTICE

Circle the correct words.

1. The word dēlēgī is the (first, second, third, fourth) principal part of the (first, second, third, third i-stem) conjugation verb dēligō.

2. The word sessum is the (first, second, third, fourth) principal part of the (first, second, third, third i-stem) conjugation verb sedeō.

3. The word dūcere is the (first, second, third, fourth) principal part of the (first, second, third, third i-stem) conjugation verb dūcō.

4. The word labōrāre is the (first, second, third, fourth) principal part of the (first, second, third, third i-stem) conjugation verb labōrō.

5. The word mānsī is the (first, second, third, fourth) principal part of the (first, second, third, third i-stem) conjugation verb maneō.

6. The word vidēre is the (first, second, third, fourth) principal part of the (first, second, third, third i-stem) conjugation verb videō.

7. The word dictum is the (first, second, third, fourth) principal part of the (first, second, third, third i-stem) conjugation verb dīcō.

8. The word parāvī is the (first, second, third, fourth) principal part of the (first, second, third, third i-stem) conjugation verb parō.

9. The word cēpī is the (first, second, third, fourth) principal part of the (first, second, third, third i-stem) conjugation verb capiō.

10. The word accipiō is the (first, second, third, fourth) principal part of the (first, second, third, third i-stem) conjugation verb accipiō.

☐ Flashcards

LET'S PRACTICE

Match the Latin sentences to their meanings.

_____ 1. Pater puerum videt.

_____ 2. Puer patrem videt.

_____ 3. Gladium capitis.

_____ 4. Gladium capis.

_____ 5. Litteram in carrō scrībimus.

_____ 6. Litteram in carrō scrībunt.

_____ 7. Rēx cōnsilium capit.*

_____ 8. Rēgēs cōnsilium capiunt.

_____ 9. In agrō hostēs sedent.

_____ 10. In agrīs hostium sedent.

_____ 11. Nōnne rēgem amat?

_____ 12. Num rēgem amat?

_____ 13. Iter saepe facis.

_____ 14. Iter saepe facitis.

_____ 15. Ubi frātrem dūcit?

_____ 16. Cūr frātrem dūcit?

_____ 17. Gentēs in vīllā manent.

_____ 18. Gēns in vīllā manet.

_____ 19. Sorōrī fābulam nārrāmus.

_____ 20. Sorōrēs fābulam nārrant.

a. The boy sees the father.

b. The father sees the boy.

c. You (sing.) take the sword.

d. You (pl.) take the sword.

e. We write a letter on the cart.

f. They write letter on the cart.

g. The kings make a plan.

h. The king makes a plan.

i. The enemies sit in the field.

j. They sit in the enemies' fields.

k. He loves the king, doesn't he?

l. He doesn't love the king, does he?

m. You (pl.) often march.

n. You (sing.) often march.

o. Where does he lead the brother?

p. Why does he lead the brother?

q. The family stays in the farmhouse.

r. The families stay in the farmhouse.

s. The sisters tell the story.

t. We tell the sister the story.

*The words cōnsilium and capiō together mean "make a plan" or "form a plan."

☐ Flashcards

Latin Workbook - Level 4
Copyright © 2000 by Karen Mohs

121

LET'S PRACTICE

Write the meanings of the Latin words. On the last set, write the Latin words.

accipiō _____

accipis _____

accipit _____

accipimus _____

accipitis _____

accipiunt _____

occupō _____

occupās _____

occupat _____

occupāmus _____

occupātis _____

occupant _____

dīcō _____

dīcis _____

dīcit _____

dīcimus _____

dīcitis _____

dīcunt _____

capiō _____

capis _____

capit _____

capimus _____

capitis _____

capiunt _____

sedeō _____

sedēs _____

sedet _____

sedēmus _____

sedētis _____

sedent _____

dēligō _____

dēligis _____

dēligit _____

dēligimus _____

dēligitis _____

dēligunt _____

I do _____

you (sing.) do _____

he (she, it) does _____

we do _____

you (pl.) do _____

they do _____

☐ Flashcards

122

Latin Workbook - Level 4
Copyright © 2000 by Karen Mohs

Lesson 28

FOURTH DECLENSION NOUNS

So far, we know three declensions of Latin nouns:

Ending of Genitive Singular	Declension
-ae	first
-ī	second
-is	third (including i-stems)

Now we learn that nouns ending in -ūs in the genitive singular belong to the *fourth declension.*

Singular

Nom.	manus	means	**the hand** (*subject of sentence*)
Gen.	manūs	means	**of the hand** (*shows possession*)
Dat.	manuī	means	**to (or for) the hand** (*indirect object*)
Acc.	manum	means	**the hand** (*direct object*)
Abl.	in manū	means	**in the hand** (*ablative of place where*)

Plural

Nom.	manūs	means	**the hands** (*subject of sentence*)
Gen.	manuum	means	**of the hands** (*shows possession*)
Dat.	manibus	means	**to (or for) the hands** (*indirect object*)
Acc.	manūs	means	**the hands** (*direct object*)
Abl.	in manibus	means	**in the hands** (*ablative of place where*)

(Remember: To find the stem of a noun, remove the genitive singular ending.)

Circle the correct words.

for the hands	of the senate	of the hands
manibus manūs	senātum senātūs	manuum manum
senates	in the hand	to the senate
senātuī senātūs senātibus	in manū in manuī in manūs	senātūs senātibus senātuī

☐ Flashcards - (Add the new cards.)

Latin Workbook - Level 4
Copyright © 2000 by Karen Mohs

LET'S PRACTICE

Put the correct endings on these Latin words.

ū is ō um	1. The man sees the king's son in the senate. Vir fīli____ rēg____ in senāt____ videt.	
is em ne ī	2. You tell the truth to the crowd, don't you? Nōn____ multitūdin____ vēritāt____ dīc____?	
at et a um	3. The queen looks at the envoy and answers. Rēgin____ lēgāt____ spect____ et respond____.	
ī en e ae	4. What is the name of the island in the sea? Quid est nōm____ īnsul____ in mar____?	
ā ō eō iō	5. Behold! I come and I fight with boldness! Ecce! Cum audāci____ ven____ et pugn____!	
iunt ant er ī	6. The lieutenants march for a long time and then attack. Lēgāt____ diū it____ fac____ et tum oppugn____.	
ēs imus um īs	7. We don't capture the enemies with swords, do we? N____ host____ gladi____ cap____?	
ōs itis ātis um	8. You receive the grain, but you do not keep the carts. Frūment____ accip____, sed carr____ nōn serv____.	
ēs um iunt ā	9. The kings and queens make a plan in the forest. Rēg____ rēginaeque in silv____ cōnsili____ cap____.	
īs āmus ās ibus	10. Afterward, we prepare the roads for the allies. Posteā soci____ vi____ par____.	

☐ Flashcards

124

Latin Workbook - Level 4
Copyright © 2000 by Karen Mohs

LET'S PRACTICE

Finish the words with the correct endings.

1. Man_____ means **of the band of men**.

2. Cōnsili_____ means **of the plans**.

3. Mort_____ means **for the death**.

4. Homin_____ means **the human beings**.

5. Itiner_____ means **of the journeys**.

6. Mar_____ means **of the seas**.

7. Vēritāt_____ means **by means of the truth**.

8. Mātr_____ means **to the mother**.

9. Nōmin_____ means **for the names**.

10. Senāt_____ means **of the senates**.

11. Host_____ means **of the enemies**.

12. Multitūdin_____ means **for the great numbers**.

13. Patr_____ means **the senators**.

14. Rēg_____ means **to the kings**.

15. Port_____ means **of the gate**.

☐ Flashcards

Latin Workbook - Level 4
Copyright © 2000 by Karen Mohs

125

LET'S PRACTICE

Write the meanings beside the Latin words.

senātus _____

senātūs _____

senātuī _____

senātum _____

in senātū _____

senātūs _____

senātuum _____

senātibus _____

senātūs _____

in senātibus _____

nōmen _____

nōminis _____

nōminī _____

nōmen _____

nōmine _____

nōmina _____

nōminum _____

nōminibus _____

nōmina _____

nōminibus _____

mare _____

maris _____

marī _____

mare _____

in marī _____

maria _____

marium _____

maribus _____

maria _____

in maribus _____

☐ Flashcards

126

Latin Workbook - Level 4
Copyright © 2000 by Karen Mohs

Lesson 29

FOURTH CONJUGATION VERBS

All regular Latin **verbs** belong to one of the four Latin conjugations.

Ending of Second Principal Part	Conjugation
-āre	first
-ēre	second
-ere	third (including i-stems)
-īre	fourth

The **present stem** of a fourth conjugation verb is found in the same way as that of first and second conjugation verbs. Simply drop the -re from the second principal part. The present stem of these verbs ends in -ī-.

Example: audiō audīre audīvī audītum
The present stem is audī-.

audiō means **I hear.**   audīmus means **We hear.**

audīs means **You** (singular) **hear.**   audītis means **You** (plural) **hear.**

audit means **He (she, it) hears.**   audiunt means **They hear.**

Match the words to their meanings.

audīs   we come upon

invenīmus   they hear

audiunt   you listen to

scit   he knows

veniō   you discover

reperītis   I come

☐ Flashcards - (Add the new cards.)

Latin Workbook - Level 4
Copyright © 2000 by Karen Mohs

127

LET'S PRACTICE

Circle the correct words.

1. The word **facere** is the (first, second, third, fourth) principal part of the (first, second, third, third i-stem, fourth) conjugation verb **faciō**.

2. The word **veniō** is the (first, second, third, fourth) principal part of the (first, second, third, third i-stem, fourth) conjugation verb **veniō**.

3. The word **inventum** is the (first, second, third, fourth) principal part of the (first, second, third, third i-stem, fourth) conjugation verb **inveniō**.

4. The word **repperī** is the (first, second, third, fourth) principal part of the (first, second, third, third i-stem, fourth) conjugation verb **reperiō**.

5. The word **sedēre** is the (first, second, third, fourth) principal part of the (first, second, third, third i-stem, fourth) conjugation verb **sedeō**.

6. The word **cōnfirmāvī** is the (first, second, third, fourth) principal part of the (first, second, third, third i-stem, fourth) conjugation verb **cōnfirmō**.

7. The word **audītum** is the (first, second, third, fourth) principal part of the (first, second, third, third i-stem, fourth) conjugation verb **audiō**.

8. The word **scrībere** is the (first, second, third, fourth) principal part of the (first, second, third, third i-stem, fourth) conjugation verb **scrībō**.

9. The word **scīvī** is the (first, second, third, fourth) principal part of the (first, second, third, third i-stem, fourth) conjugation verb **sciō**.

10. The word **respondī** is the (first, second, third, fourth) principal part of the (first, second, third, third i-stem, fourth) conjugation verb **respondeō**.

☐ Flashcards

LET'S PRACTICE

Match the Latin words to their meanings.

_____	1. reperīs	a.	they find
_____	2. reperiunt	b.	we find
_____	3. reperiō	c.	you (pl.) find
_____	4. reperīmus	d.	you (sing.) find
_____	5. reperītis	e.	he (she, it) finds
_____	6. reperit	f.	I find
_____	7. accipit	g.	you (sing.) receive
_____	8. accipiō	h.	he (she, it) receives
_____	9. accipitis	i.	we receive
_____	10. accipis	j.	you (pl.) receive
_____	11. accipiunt	k.	I receive
_____	12. accipimus	l.	they receive
_____	13. inveniunt	m.	he (she, it) comes upon
_____	14. invenit	n.	you (sing.) come upon
_____	15. invenītis	o.	we come upon
_____	16. invenīs	p.	I come upon
_____	17. invenīmus	q.	you (pl.) come upon
_____	18. inveniō	r.	they come upon
_____	19. manētis	s.	you (pl.) remain
_____	20. manet	t.	you (sing.) remain
_____	21. maneō	u.	he (she, it) remains
_____	22. manent	v.	they remain
_____	23. manēmus	w.	I remain
_____	24. manēs	x.	we remain

☐ Flashcards

Latin Workbook - Level 4
Copyright © 2000 by Karen Mohs

129

LET'S PRACTICE

Write the meanings of the Latin words. On the last set, write the Latin words.

sciō _____	scīmus _____
scīs _____	scītis _____
scit _____	sciunt _____
inveniō _____	invenīmus _____
invenīs _____	invenītis _____
invenit _____	inveniunt _____
pugnō _____	pugnāmus _____
pugnās _____	pugnātis _____
pugnat _____	pugnant _____
videō _____	vidēmus _____
vidēs _____	vidētis _____
videt _____	vident _____
superō _____	superāmus _____
superās _____	superātis _____
superat _____	superant _____
audiō _____	audīmus _____
audīs _____	audītus _____
audit _____	audiunt _____
I come _____	we come _____
you (sing.) come _____	you (pl.) come _____
he (she, it) comes _____	they come _____

☐ Flashcards

130

Latin Workbook - Level 4
Copyright © 2000 by Karen Mohs

Lesson 30

FIFTH DECLENSION NOUNS

All regular Latin **nouns** belong to one of the five Latin declensions.

Ending of Genitive Singular	Declension
-ae	first
-ī	second
-is	third (including i-stems)
-ūs	fourth
-ēī or -eī*	fifth

Nouns ending in -ēī or -eī in the genitive singular belong to the *fifth declension*.

Singular

Nom.	diēs	means	**the day**	spēs	means	**the hope**
Gen.	diēī	means	**of the day**	speī	means	**of the hope**
Dat.	diēī	means	**to (or for) the day**	speī	means	**to (or for) the hope**
Acc.	diem	means	**the day**	spem	means	**the hope**
Abl.	diē	means	**by means of the day**	spē	means	**by means of the hope**

Plural

Nom.	diēs	means	**the days**	spēs	means	**the hopes**
Gen.	diērum	means	**of the days**	spērum	means	**of the hopes**
Dat.	diēbus	means	**to (or for) the days**	spēbus	means	**to (or for) the hopes**
Acc.	diēs	means	**the days**	spēs	means	**the hopes**
Abl.	diēbus	means	**by means of the days**	spēbus	means	**by means of the hopes**

(Remember: To find the stem of a noun, remove the genitive singular ending.)

Write the words on the right under the correct headings.

fourth declension	fifth declension
_ _ _ _ _ _ _ _ _ _ _ _ _ _	_ _ _ _ _ _ _ _ _ _ _ _ _ _
_____	_____
_____	_____
_____	_____

fidēs
manus
senātus
spēs

*The fifth declension ending is actually -ī. The -ē- (or -e- if after a consonant and before a vowel) is the stem ending. However, it is easy to recognize this declension by the -ēī or -eī of the genitive singular.

☐ Flashcards - (Add the new cards.)

Latin Workbook - Level 4
Copyright © 2000 by Karen Mohs

131

LET'S PRACTICE

Circle the correct words.

spēs	hope for the hopes of the hope	fideī	faith of the faith for the faiths
senātuī	of the senate senates to the senate	marī	seas for the sea of the sea
fidēs	of the faith faiths for the faiths	diem	days day of the days
itinerum	routes route of the routes	manuum	of the hands for the hand hand
fidē	by means of faith of the faith for the faith	nōmina	in the name name names
diērum	for the days of the days days	spēbus	of the hopes hopes for the hopes
speī	for the hope hopes of the hopes	urbium	city of the cities of the city

☐ Flashcards

132

LET'S PRACTICE

Circle the correct genders (**m** for *masculine*, **f** for *feminine*, **n** for *neuter*).
Circle the correct declensions (**1st** for *first declension*, **2nd** for *second declension*, **3rd** for *third declension*, **3rd-I** for *third declension i-stem*, **4th** for *fourth declension*, and **5th** for *fifth declension*).

nautae	m	f	n	1st	2nd	3rd	3rd-I	4th	5th
itinera	m	f	n	1st	2nd	3rd	3rd-I	4th	5th
diēī	m	f	n	1st	2nd	3rd	3rd-I	4th	5th
marī	m	f	n	1st	2nd	3rd	3rd-I	4th	5th
rēgis	m	f	n	1st	2nd	3rd	3rd-I	4th	5th
mortem	m	f	n	1st	2nd	3rd	3rd-I	4th	5th
manūs	m	f	n	1st	2nd	3rd	3rd-I	4th	5th
agrōrum	m	f	n	1st	2nd	3rd	3rd-I	4th	5th
urbe	m	f	n	1st	2nd	3rd	3rd-I	4th	5th
puerī	m	f	n	1st	2nd	3rd	3rd-I	4th	5th
nōmine	m	f	n	1st	2nd	3rd	3rd-I	4th	5th
terrās	m	f	n	1st	2nd	3rd	3rd-I	4th	5th
spēbus	m	f	n	1st	2nd	3rd	3rd-I	4th	5th
mātribus	m	f	n	1st	2nd	3rd	3rd-I	4th	5th
maria	m	f	n	1st	2nd	3rd	3rd-I	4th	5th
hostēs	m	f	n	1st	2nd	3rd	3rd-I	4th	5th
senātibus	m	f	n	1st	2nd	3rd	3rd-I	4th	5th
verbō	m	f	n	1st	2nd	3rd	3rd-I	4th	5th
gentium	m	f	n	1st	2nd	3rd	3rd-I	4th	5th

☐ Flashcards

Latin Workbook - Level 4
Copyright © 2000 by Karen Mohs

LET'S PRACTICE

Write the meanings beside the Latin words.

fidēs _____   fidēs _____

fideī _____   fidērum _____

fideī _____   fidēbus _____

fidem _____   fidēs _____

fidē _____   fidēbus _____

---

homō _____   hominēs _____

hominis _____   hominum _____

hominī _____   hominibus _____

hominem _____   hominēs _____

cum homine _____   cum hominibus _____

---

diēs _____   diēs _____

diēī _____   diērum _____

diēī _____   diēbus _____

diem _____   diēs _____

diē _____   diēbus _____

☐ Flashcards

LET'S PRACTICE

Choose the best words for the sentences below. Put them in the blanks.
Write what the sentences mean.

sedeō	gladiōsque	fēminae

1. Aquam _____ nunc dēligō.

   It means _____

2. Frāterne _____ in campō semper labōrat?

   It means _____

3. Cum audāciā in carrō dominī hodiē _____.

   It means _____

---

esne	sumus	est

1. Vir rēgīnae _____ rēx patriae.

   It means _____

2. _____ māter fīlī fīliaeque in silvā?

   It means _____

3. Amīcī _____, sed populum tubā nōn convocāmus.

   It means _____

☐ Flashcards

LET'S PRACTICE

Finish the words with the correct endings.

1. Cum amīciti_____ means **with friendliness.**

2. Nōmin_____ means **for the names.**

3. Sorōr_____ means **sisters.**

4. Numer_____ means **of the group.**

5. Man_____ means **to the hand.**

6. Vi_____ means **of the roads.**

7. Sp_____ means **hope** (*direct object*).

8. Cōnsil_____ means **of the advice.**

9. Senāt_____ means **of the senates.**

10. Gent_____ means **families.**

11. Vēritāt_____ means **for the truths.**

12. Mar_____ means **seas.**

13. Loc_____ means **for the situation.**

14. Urb_____ means **of the city.**

15. Fid_____ means **for the loyalty.**

☐ Flashcards

LET'S PRACTICE

Write the words on the right under the correct headings.

first declension	second declension

third declension	third declension i-stem

fifth declension

fourth declension

agricola
animus
diēs
fāma
fidēs
frūmentum
fuga
gēns
homō
hostis
iter
manus
mare
māter
memoria
mors
nōmen
rēx
senātus
spēs
urbs
verbum
vēritās
vir

☐ Flashcards

Latin Workbook - Level 4
Copyright © 2000 by Karen Mohs

137

LET'S PRACTICE

Write the verbs in Latin.

he writes _____

she hears _____

they know _____

I sit _____

you (pl.) discover _____

they remain _____

we make _____

you (sing.) answer _____

we come upon _____

she chooses _____

they take _____

they lead _____

you (sing.) come _____

you (sing.) receive _____

we shout _____

you (pl.) say _____

☐ Flashcards

Lesson 31

ergō

means

therefore, then

Write the Latin word that means **therefore**.

Write the Latin word that means **I judge**.

iūdicō

iūdicāre iūdicāvī iūdicātum

means

I judge, I consider

oppidum

oppidī (neuter)

means

town

Write the Latin word that means **town**.

☐ Flashcards - (Add the new cards.)

Latin Workbook - Level 4
Copyright © 2000 by Karen Mohs

139

LET'S PRACTICE

Circle the English meanings of the Latin words.

senātus	senator	congress	senate
pater	sound	father	cloth
reperiō	repair	gather	I discover
ergō	therefore	fine	spine
capiō	I take	I cut	I improve
vēritās	old	extra	trueness
accipiō	I trip	I accept	I stress
ecce	ouch	behold	inch
audiō	I listen to	I dare	I play
iūdicō	I tease	I juggle	I consider
inveniō	I come upon	I study	I make
manus	jaw	smell	hand
diēs	day	god	stand
oppidum	chance	town	medicine
fidēs	pledge	dog	flame
iter	itch	route	item
multitūdō	arena	couch	crowd
cōnsilium	apology	foresight	surrender
spēs	animal	hope	kind
sciō	I know	I sing	I climb
homō	mixture	man	milk

☐ Flashcards

140

Latin Workbook - Level 4
Copyright © 2000 by Karen Mohs

quōmodo

means

how?

Write the Latin word that means **how?**

Write the Latin word that means **law**.

lēx
lēgis (feminine)

means

law

dōnum
dōnī (neuter)

means

gift, present

Write the Latin word that means **gift**.

☐ Flashcards - (Add the new cards.)

Latin Workbook - Level 4
Copyright © 2000 by Karen Mohs

141

LET'S PRACTICE

Circle the correct words.

gift	pater iter dōnum	name	fidēs nōmen homō
mother	māter manus nōmen	death	diēs mors māter
law	rēx mare lēx	how?	spēs quōmodo ecce
therefore	sed et ergō	I stay	accipiō maneō reperiō
I sit	sedeō dīcō scrībō	I come	videō dūcō veniō
I do	dō respondeō faciō	I consider	audiō iūdicō dēligō
town	gēns oppidum urbs	I choose	dēligō faciō maneō

□ Flashcards

142

Latin Workbook - Level 4
Copyright © 2000 by Karen Mohs

Lesson 32

magister

magistrī (masculine)

means

master, teacher, director

Write the Latin word that means **teacher**.

Write the Latin word that means **leader**.

dux

ducis (masculine)

means

leader, guide

animal

animālis (neuter)

means

animal

Write the Latin word that means **animal**.

☐ Flashcards - (Add the new cards.)

Latin Workbook - Level 4
Copyright © 2000 by Karen Mohs

143

LET'S PRACTICE

Match the words to their meanings.

male	badly
quid	how?
quōmodo	what?
amīcus	animal
animī	courage
animal	friend
oppidum	I attack
oppugnō	town
occupō	I seize
magister	owner
dominus	place
locus	teacher
crās	therefore
lēx	tomorrow
ergō	law
inopia	lack
iūdicō	meanwhile
interim	I consider
dux	long
dōnum	present
diū	leader

☐ Flashcards

144

habeō
habēre habuī habitum

means

**I have, I hold,
I keep, I consider**

Write the Latin word that means **I have**.

Write the Latin word that means **I put**.

pōnō
pōnere posuī positum

means

**I put, I set,
I place, I locate**

lapis
lapidis (masculine)

means

stone

Write the Latin word that means **stone**.

☐ Flashcards - (Add the new cards.)

Latin Workbook - Level 4
Copyright © 2000 by Karen Mohs

145

LET'S PRACTICE

Match the Latin words to their meanings.

_____	1. ubi	a. how?
_____	2. saepe	b. always
_____	3. quōmodo	c. therefore
_____	4. quid	d. why?
_____	5. cūr	e. where?
_____	6. semper	f. what?
_____	7. ergō	g. often
_____	8. nunc	h. now
_____	9. pōnō	i. I sit
_____	10. iūdicō	j. I have
_____	11. sedeō	k. I put
_____	12. inveniō	l. I capture
_____	13. habeō	m. I come
_____	14. veniō	n. I judge
_____	15. capiō	o. I find
_____	16. sciō	p. I know
_____	17. magister	q. grain
_____	18. lēx	r. gift
_____	19. animal	s. town
_____	20. oppidum	t. guide
_____	21. lapis	u. master
_____	22. dōnum	v. stone
_____	23. frūmentum	w. animal
_____	24. dux	x. law

☐ Flashcards

146

Latin Workbook - Level 4
Copyright © 2000 by Karen Mohs

Lesson 33

adventus
adventūs (masculine)
means
arrival, approach

Write the Latin word that means **arrival**.

Write the Latin word that means **I surrender**.

trādō
trādere trādidī trāditum
means
**I hand over, I surrender,
I hand down**

iaciō
iacere iēcī iactum
means
I throw

Write the Latin word that means **I throw**.

☐ Flashcards - (Add the new cards.)

Latin Workbook - Level 4
Copyright © 2000 by Karen Mohs

147

LET'S PRACTICE

Write the meanings of the following Latin words.

hostis _____

trādō _____

lapis _____

dux _____

maneō _____

iūdicō _____

urbs _____

magister _____

quōmodo _____

mors _____

adventus _____

ecce _____

caelum _____

habeō _____

oppidum _____

iaciō _____

ergō _____

nōmen _____

dōnum _____

scrībō _____

pōnō _____

lēx _____

diēs _____

animal _____

accipiō _____

☐ Flashcards

148

Latin Workbook - Level 4
Copyright © 2000 by Karen Mohs

portus

portūs (masculine)

means

harbor, port

Write the Latin word that means **harbor**.

Write the Latin word that means **power**.

potestās

potestātis (feminine)

means

power, opportunity

regō

regere rēxī rēctum

means

I rule

Write the Latin word that means **I rule**.

☐ Flashcards - (Add the new cards.)

Latin Workbook - Level 4
Copyright © 2000 by Karen Mohs

149

LET'S PRACTICE

Write the correct Latin verbs, including all four principal parts.

I know

I throw

I attempt

I hear

I rule

I judge

I take

I hold

I receive

I prepare

I surrender

I come

I discover

I come
upon

I set

I fly

☐ Flashcards

150

Latin Workbook - Level 4
Copyright © 2000 by Karen Mohs

LET'S PRACTICE

Circle the correct words.

for the arrival	adventūs adventuī adventū	of the laws	lēgōrum lēgium lēgum
they rule	regent regunt regiunt	we consider	habīmus habimus habēmus
leaders	ducēs ducae ducī	they throw	iacunt iaciunt iacent
you locate	pōnīs pōnis pōnēs	stone	lapēs lapidis lapis
the animals	animālia animāla animālēs	for the powers	potestātīs potestātibus potestātum
of the ports	portibus portuum portūs	of the director	magistrī magistuī magistūs
presents	dōnī dōnēs dōna	you hand over	trādātis trāditis trādētis

☐ Flashcards

Latin Workbook - Level 4
Copyright © 2000 by Karen Mohs

151

LET'S PRACTICE

Write the correct Latin verbs.

1. _____ is the **third** principal part of sedeō.

2. _____ is the **second** principal part of reperiō.

3. _____ is the **fourth** principal part of iūdicō.

4. _____ is the **first** principal part of vulnerō.

5. _____ is the **second** principal part of iaciō.

6. _____ is the **fourth** principal part of inveniō.

7. _____ is the **third** principal part of pōnō.

8. _____ is the **fourth** principal part of capiō.

9. _____ is the **third** principal part of faciō.

10. _____ is the **second** principal part of trādō.

11. _____ is the **fourth** principal part of accipiō.

12. _____ is the **third** principal part of habeō.

13. _____ is the **second** principal part of labōrō.

14. _____ is the **third** principal part of sciō.

15. _____ is the **first** principal part of regō.

☐ Flashcards

152

Latin Workbook - Level 4
Copyright © 2000 by Karen Mohs

LET'S PRACTICE

Write these sentences in Latin.

1. Does the king rule the native land with power?

2. Why do the leaders and the men surrender the harbor?

3. The teacher hears the arrival of the carts.

4. The boys and girls throw stones.

5. How does the animal put the gift on the road?

6. They have power, but they do not lead.

7. Behold! The guide always sits in the town.

☐ Flashcards

Latin Workbook - Level 4
Copyright © 2000 by Karen Mohs

PUZZLE TIME!

Find eighteen Latin words in the puzzle below.

a	t	r	ā	d	ō	g	l	o	p	p	i	d	u	m	t	h	z	l	m	f	t
f	g	h	q	u	ō	m	o	d	o	n	g	a	x	m	a	g	i	s	t	e	r
m	l	p	s	a	n	h	ū	r	r	r	m	s	m	x	n	t	h	x	r	z	p
t	v	t	r	x	v	o	p	o	t	e	s	t	ā	s	ō	n	ū	l	s	l	o
i	ū	d	i	c	ō	m	s	x	u	p	t	l	t	p	m	a	n	i	m	a	l
a	c	c	i	p	i	ō	p	h	s	e	r	f	e	z	e	s	g	r	a	p	s
c	s	g	r	v	l	r	f	v	s	r	a	ō	r	s	n	r	o	m	n	i	g
i	n	v	p	f	z	m	x	n	p	i	m	ō	a	d	v	e	n	t	u	s	t
ō	h	m	u	l	t	i	t	ū	d	ō	t	h	g	p	f	n	m	z	s	v	h

Write the words you found. Remember to include the macrons.

1. _____   10. _____

2. _____   11. _____

3. _____   12. _____

4. _____   13. _____

5. _____   14. _____

6. _____   15. _____

7. _____   16. _____

8. _____   17. _____

9. _____   18. _____

☐ Flashcards

154

Latin Workbook - Level 4
Copyright © 2000 by Karen Mohs

Lesson 34

LET'S PRACTICE

Circle the best words. Write what the sentences mean.

1. Posteā (nautae, nautī) aquam frūmentumque in portū (pōniunt, pōnunt).

   It means _____

2. Num (magistrēs, magistrī) puerīs epistulās (iacunt, iaciunt)?

   It means _____

3. Fīliae rēgis (animālia, animālēs) tubā saepe (dūcunt, dūcent).

   It means _____

4. (Ducēsne, Ducēsque) patriam et senātum (ament, amant)?

   It means _____

5. Quōmodo nautae (iter, interum) in aquā (facunt, faciunt)?

   It means _____

6. Cūr fēminae (in vīllīs, cum vīlla) ergō (sedent, sedunt)?

   It means _____

7. Patrēs (regītis, regitis), sed captīvōs nōn (iūdicātis, iūdicētis).

   It means _____

8. Quid (hostis, hostēs) rēgis rēgīnaeque nunc (dēligent, dēligunt)?

   It means _____

9. In oppidō (in īnsulā, in īnsulō) in marī (habitās, habitēs).

   It means _____

10. Lēgēs (urbum, urbium) scīmus, et cōnsilia hodiē (capimus, capīmus).

    It means _____

☐ Flashcards

Latin Workbook - Level 4
Copyright © 2000 by Karen Mohs

155

LET'S PRACTICE

Match the Latin sentences to their meanings.

_____ 1. Rēx urbem trādit.

_____ 2. Rēgēs urbem trādunt.

_____ 3. Num puellam amat?

_____ 4. Nōnne puellam amat?

_____ 5. Estne fīlia rēgīnae?

_____ 6. Suntne fīliae rēgīnae?

_____ 7. Lapidēs in carrō habet.

_____ 8. Lapidēs in carrō habēs.

_____ 9. Nauta est in marī.

_____ 10. Nauta es in marī.

_____ 11. Cūr gladium portat?

_____ 12. Quōmodo gladium portat?

_____ 13. Virōs fīliōsque habēmus.

_____ 14. Fīliī virōs nōn habent.

_____ 15. Ducī dōna dant.

_____ 16. Dōna ducis dant.

_____ 17. Animālia captīvōs vident.

_____ 18. Animālia captīvī vident.

_____ 19. Fidem spemque habēs.

_____ 20. Fidem spemque habet.

a. The king surrenders the city.

b. The kings surrender the city.

c. He loves the girl, doesn't he?

d. He doesn't love the girl, does he?

e. Are they the queen's daughters?

f. Is she the queen's daughter?

g. He keeps stones in the wagon.

h. You keep stones in the wagon.

i. The sailor is in the sea.

j. You are the sailor in the sea.

k. How does she carry the sword?

l. Why does she carry the sword?

m. Sons do not have husbands.

n. We have husbands and sons.

o. They give the gifts of the guide.

p. They give the gifts to the guide.

q. The animals see the captives.

r. The captive's animals see.

s. You have faith and hope.

t. She has faith and hope.

☐ Flashcards

156

Latin Workbook - Level 4
Copyright © 2000 by Karen Mohs

LET'S PRACTICE

Write the meanings of the Latin sentences on the lines beneath the sentences.

Verbum dominī audītis.	Rēgem in caelō videt.
_____	_____
Dominus verba audit.	Rēgēs vident caelum.
_____	_____
Soror filiō dōna dat.	Quōmodo epistulam scrībis?
_____	_____
Fīliī sorōrī dōna dant.	Ubi epistulam scrībimus?
_____	_____
Iter in silvā rēgīnae facit.	Num pecūniam inveniunt?
_____	_____
Rēgīnae iter in silvīs faciunt.	Nōnne pecūniam invenit?
_____	_____
Senātuī vēritātem dīcō.	Mors hostibus venit.
_____	_____
Senātus vēritātem nunc scit.	Hostēs mortem nōn amant.
_____	_____
Ecce! Māter cōnsilium capit.	Ducēs lēgem oppidī iūdicant.
_____	_____
Ergō mātrēs cōnsilia capiunt.	Lēx ducēs oppidī iūdicat.
_____	_____

☐ Flashcards

Latin Workbook - Level 4
Copyright © 2000 by Karen Mohs

LET'S PRACTICE

Draw lines to connect the parts of the sentences.

1. Virīne veniunt   urbis hostibus portūs trādunt.

2. Quōmodo puer   habētis?

3. Ducēs   et puellam reperiunt?

4. Nōnne fidem   animālium amātis.

5. Nōmina   gladiōs in equīs pōnit?

Now write the sentences you have made. First write them in Latin. Then write what they mean.

1. _____

   It means _____

2. _____

   It means _____

3. _____

   It means _____

4. _____

   It means _____

5. _____

   It means _____

☐ Flashcards

158

Latin Workbook - Level 4
Copyright © 2000 by Karen Mohs

LET'S PRACTICE

Circle the correct Latin sentences. Watch for incorrect endings.

The farmers see the sailors.	Agricolae nautās vidant. Agricolae nautās vident. Agricolae nautās vidiunt.
You know the truth of the word.	Scis vēritātem verbī. Scēs vēritātem verbī. Scīs vēritātem verbī.
The poets always write letters.	Poētae litterās semper scrībunt. Poētī litterās semper scrībunt. Poētēs litterās semper scrībunt.
The animals live in the sea.	Animālia in marī habitant. Animālia in marō habitant. Animālia in mare habitant.
The sisters carry the grain.	Sorōrae frūmentum portant. Sorōra frūmentum portant. Sorōrēs frūmentum portant.
You give the presents to the family.	Gentae dōna datis. Gentī dōna datis. Gentis dōna datis.
Men and women are human beings.	Virī fēminaeque sunt hominōs. Virī fēminaeque sunt hominēs. Virī fēminaeque sunt homēs.
We receive swords and horses.	Gladiōs equōsque accipimus. Gladiōs equōsque accipēmus. Gladiōs equōsque accipīmus.

☐ Flashcards

Latin Workbook - Level 4
Copyright © 2000 by Karen Mohs

LET'S PRACTICE

Read these Latin sentences. Write what they mean.

1. Quōmodo adventus lēgātōrum rēgis spem donat?

   It means _____

2. Nōnne sociī rēgī pecūniam in viā iaciunt?

   It means _____

3. Ergō nunc numerus animālium in caelō saepe volant.

   It means _____

4. Hostēs filiō ducis lapidēs in marī dēmōnstrant.

   It means _____

5. In urbe nunc sum, sed in villā in oppidō habitō.

   It means _____

6. Ducēsne nūntiōs lēgātōrum iam exspectant?

   It means _____

7. Captīvōs tubā saepe convocātis.

   It means _____

8. Num servus magistrum reperit et lapidēs iacit?

   It means _____

9. Cūr frātrēs sorōrēsque in lūdō pugnant?

   It means _____

10. Nōnne dominī servōs hodiē liberant?

    It means _____

☐ Flashcards

160

Latin Workbook - Level 4
Copyright © 2000 by Karen Mohs

Lesson 35

FINAL REVIEW

Write the meanings of the following Latin words.

potestās _____

vulnerō _____

caelum _____

frūmentum _____

mors _____

videō _____

lingua _____

portus _____

dēligō _____

habitō _____

tuba _____

maneō _____

diēs _____

ubi _____

dōnum _____

homō _____

occupō _____

accipiō _____

causa _____

audiō _____

habeō _____

trādō _____

nātūra _____

cōnsilium _____

iūdicō _____

faciō _____

crās _____

verbum _____

lapis _____

pater _____

equus _____

nōmen _____

frāter _____

quōmodo _____

soror _____

quid _____

pōnō _____

ergō _____

iter _____

stō _____

dīcō _____

rēx _____

☐ Flashcards

Latin Workbook - Level 4
Copyright © 2000 by Karen Mohs

161

FINAL REVIEW

Write the meanings of the following Latin words.

multitūdō _____

hostis _____

vēritās _____

dux _____

poena _____

scrībō _____

sunt _____

adventus _____

manus _____

respondeō _____

reperiō _____

campus _____

fuga _____

animal _____

sciō _____

sedeō _____

dūcō _____

interim _____

magister _____

clāmō _____

gēns _____

fābula _____

herī _____

regō _____

inveniō _____

māter _____

mare _____

capiō _____

iam _____

oppidum _____

hōra _____

ecce _____

vir _____

fidēs _____

lēx _____

senātus _____

dīligentia _____

urbs _____

animus _____

iaciō _____

spēs _____

veniō _____

☐ Flashcards

162

Latin Workbook - Level 4
Copyright © 2000 by Karen Mohs

FINAL REVIEW

Label the three final Latin syllables.

po　　tes　　tā　　tis

_____　_____　_____　_____

Write the words in the box under the correct headings. (Words will be used more than once.)

| adventūs | iūdicāvī | potestās |
| animālia | lapidem | quōmodo |

short antepenult　　　　long antepenult　　　　short penult

long penult　　　　short ultima　　　　long ultima

Divide the words correctly by drawing vertical lines between the syllables.

adventus　　　habētis　　　senātuī　　　hominis

oppidōrum　　　regere　　　reperīre　　　cōnsilī

magistrōs　　　multitūdinis　　　diēī　　　nōmine

☐ Flashcards

Latin Workbook - Level 4
Copyright © 2000 by Karen Mohs

163

FINAL REVIEW

Write the meanings beside the Latin words.

The "being" verb

sum _____   sumus _____

es _____   estis _____

est _____   sunt _____

First declension

nauta _____   nautae _____

nautae _____   nautārum _____

nautae _____   nautīs _____

nautam _____   nautās _____

cum nautā _____   cum nautīs _____

First conjugation

habitō _____   habitāmus _____

habitās _____   habitātis _____

habitat _____   habitant _____

Second declension -us

lūdus _____   lūdī _____

lūdī _____   lūdōrum _____

lūdō _____   lūdīs _____

lūdum _____   lūdōs _____

in lūdō _____   in lūdīs _____

☐ Flashcards

164

Latin Workbook - Level 4
Copyright © 2000 by Karen Mohs

FINAL REVIEW

Write the meanings beside the Latin words.

Second declension -ius

socius _____   sociī _____

socī _____   sociōrum _____

sociō _____   sociīs _____

socium _____   sociōs _____

cum sociō _____   cum sociīs _____

Second declension -er

magister _____   magistrī _____

magistrī _____   magistrōrum _____

magistrō _____   magistrīs _____

magistrum _____   magistrōs _____

cum magistrō _____   cum magistrīs _____

Second declension neuter

dōnum _____   dōna _____

dōnī _____   dōnōrum _____

dōnō _____   dōnīs _____

dōnum _____   dōna _____

in dōnō _____   in dōnīs _____

Second conjugation

habeō _____   habēmus _____

habēs _____   habētis _____

habet _____   habent _____

□ Flashcards

Latin Workbook - Level 4
Copyright © 2000 by Karen Mohs

165

Lesson 36

FINAL REVIEW

Write the meanings beside the Latin words.

Third conjugation

regō	_____	regimus	_____
regis	_____	regitis	_____
regit	_____	regunt	_____

Third conjugation i-stem

iaciō	_____	iacimus	_____
iacis	_____	iacitis	_____
iacit	_____	iaciunt	_____

Third declension

lapis	_____	lapidēs	_____
lapidis	_____	lapidum	_____
lapidī	_____	lapidibus	_____
lapidem	_____	lapidēs	_____
lapide	_____	lapidibus	_____

Third declension neuter

iter	_____	itinera	_____
itineris	_____	itinerum	_____
itinerī	_____	itineribus	_____
iter	_____	itinera	_____
itinere	_____	itineribus	_____

☐ Flashcards

166

Latin Workbook - Level 4
Copyright © 2000 by Karen Mohs

FINAL REVIEW

Write the meanings beside the Latin words.

Third declension i-stem

urbs _____   urbēs _____

urbis _____   urbium _____

urbī _____   urbibus _____

urbem _____   urbēs _____

in urbe _____   in urbibus _____

Third declension i-stem neuter

animal _____   animālia _____

animālis _____   animālium _____

animālī _____   animālibus _____

animal _____   animālia _____

cum animālī _____   cum animālibus _____

Fourth declension

portus _____   portūs _____

portūs _____   portuum _____

portuī _____   portibus _____

portum _____   portūs _____

in portū _____   in portibus _____

Fourth conjugation

reperiō _____   reperīmus _____

reperīs _____   reperītis _____

reperit _____   reperiunt _____

☐ Flashcards

Latin Workbook - Level 4
Copyright © 2000 by Karen Mohs

167

FINAL REVIEW

Write the meanings beside the Latin words.

Fifth declension

spēs _____   spēs _____

speī _____   spērum _____

speī _____   spēbus _____

spem _____   spēs _____

spē _____   spēbus _____

Write these sentences in Latin.

1. The leader of the senate stays with the boys.

   _____

   _____

2. The king's lieutenant fights with a sword.

   _____

   _____

3. You (singular) write the letters with care, don't you?

   _____

   _____

4. The captives seize the farmer's field.

   _____

   _____

5. The death of the horse does not please the ally, does it?

   _____

   _____

☐ Flashcards

168

Latin Workbook - Level 4
Copyright © 2000 by Karen Mohs

FINAL REVIEW

Read these Latin sentences. Write what they mean.

1. Cūr frātrēs amīcīs sorōris fābulam saepe nārrant?

   It means _____

2. Ergō rēgis potestās vēritāsque gentī spem dant.

   It means _____

3. Num populus urbium frūmentum in equīs pōnit?

   It means _____

4. Puerīne adventum hostium patriae audiunt?

   It means _____

5. Posteā cōnsilia ducum in portā magistrī invenīmus.

   It means _____

6. Patris animālia gladiō oppugnātis et vulnerātis.

   It means _____

7. Quōmodo cum dīligentiā in agrō agricolae diū labōrās?

   It means _____

8. Nōnne māter rēgīnae fidem gentium scit?

   It means _____

9. Manūs iter in oppidō faciunt et multitūdinem regunt.

   It means _____

10. Ecce! Nōmen urbis lēge iūdicāmus.

    It means _____

□ Flashcards

Latin Workbook - Level 4
Copyright © 2000 by Karen Mohs

PUZZLE TIME!

Think of the meaning of the English word. Write the Latin word on the puzzle below.

across

1. truth
4. mind
8. father
10. I grant
14. sea
15. harbor
16. how?
17. I stand
18. stone
20. guide
21. to
22. I rule
23. grain
26. director
27. I discover
30. brother
33. approach
34. behold
35. I say
36. king
37. therefore

down

1. husband
2. hope
3. I come
4. I receive
5. already
6. often
7. present
9. sky
11. human being
12. I hand down
13. name
15. power
17. sister
19. I look at
21. animal
24. I write
25. I have
28. I locate
29. journey
31. but
32. law
34. and

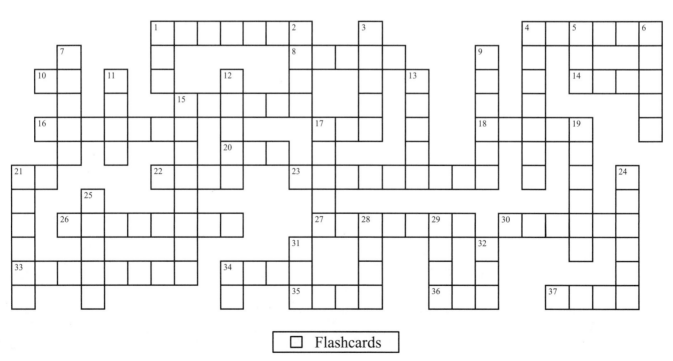

☐ Flashcards

170

Latin Workbook - Level 4
Copyright © 2000 by Karen Mohs

APPENDIX

Latin - English Glossary

a

accipiō, accipere, accēpī, acceptum - I receive, I accept (99)

ad - to, near, toward, for, at (8)

adventus, adventūs (m.) - arrival, approach (147)

ager, agrī (m.) - field, territory (11)

agricola, agricolae (m.) - farmer (7)

ambulō, ambulāre, ambulāvī, ambulātum - I stroll, I walk (24)

amīcitia, amīcitiae (f.) - friendship, friendliness (13)

amīcus, amīcī (m.) - friend (11)

amō, amāre, amāvī, amātum - I love, I like (13)

animal, animālis (n.) - animal (143)

animus, animī (m.) - mind, spirit; (pl., courage) (21)

annus, annī (m.) - year (14)

appellō, appellāre, appellāvī, appellātum - I address, I call, I name (15)

aqua, aquae (f.) - water (7)

audācia, audāciae (f.) - boldness, daring (21)

audiō, audīre, audīvī, audītum - I hear, I listen to (93)

c

caelum, caelī (n.) - sky, heavens (49)

campus, campī (m.) - field, plain (12)

capiō, capere, cēpī, captum - I take, I capture (95); cōnsilium capiō - I form (make) a plan (121)

captīvus, captīvī (m.) - captive, prisoner (21)

carrus, carrī (m.) - cart, wagon (22)

causa, causae (f.) - cause, reason (18)

clāmō, clāmāre, clāmāvī, clāmātum - I shout (24)

cōnfirmō, cōnfirmāre, cōnfirmāvī, cōnfirmātum - I strengthen, I encourage, I declare (24)

cōnsilium, cōnsilī (n.) - plan, advice, foresight (99); cōnsilium capiō - I form (make) a plan (121)

convocō, convocāre, convocāvī, convocātum - I call together, I assemble, I summon (18)

cōpia, cōpiae (f.) - plenty, supply; (pl., troops, forces) (19)

crās - tomorrow (22)

cum - along with, with (12)

cūr - why? (23)

cūra, cūrae (f.) - care, anxiety (22)

d

dēlectō, dēlectāre, dēlectāvī, dēlectātum - I please (17)

dēligō, dēligere, dēlēgī, dēlēctum - I choose (59)

dēmōnstrō, dēmōnstrāre, dēmōnstrāvī, dēmōnstrātum - I point out, I show (23)

dīcō, dīcere, dīxī, dictum - I say, I tell (53)

d

diēs, diēī (m. & f.) - day (93)

dīligentia, dīligentiae (f.) - diligence, care (18)

diū - for a long time, long (19)

dō, dare, dedī, datum - I give, I grant (9)

dominus, dominī (m.) - master, lord, owner (24)

dōnum, dōnī (n.) - gift, present (141)

dūcō, dūcere, dūxī, ductum - I lead, I bring (55)

dux, ducis (m.) - leader, guide (143)

e

ecce - behold (103)

epistula, epistulae (f.) - letter, epistle (17)

equus, equī (m.) - horse (14)

ergō - therefore, then (139)

est - he is, she is, it is, there is (8)

et - and, also, even (8)

exspectō, exspectāre, exspectāvī, exspectātum - I await, I wait for (17)

f

fābula, fābulae (f.) - story (17)

faciō, facere, fēcī, factum - I make, I do (91); iter faciō - I march (110)

fāma, fāmae (f.) - report, rumor, reputation (16)

fēmina, fēminae (f.) - woman, wife (7)

fidēs, fideī (f.) - faith, loyalty, pledge, confidence (97)

Note: The number in parentheses indicates the page on which the vocabulary word is introduced.

Latin Workbook - Level 4
Copyright © 2000 by Karen Mohs

171

APPENDIX

Latin - English Glossary

filia, filiae (f.) - daughter (13)
filius, fīlī (m.) - son (13)
fortūna, fortūnae (f.) - fortune, chance, luck (10)
frāter, frātris (m.) - brother (55)
frūmentum, frūmentī (n.) - grain (57)
fuga, fugae (f.) - flight, exile (19)

g
gēns, gentis (f.) - nation, family, clan (53)
gladius, gladī (m.) - sword (15)

h
habeō, habēre, habuī, habitum - I have, I hold, I keep, I consider (145)
habitō, habitāre, habitāvī, habitātum - I live, I dwell (17)
herī - yesterday (20)
hodiē - today (21)
homō, hominis (m. or f.) - human being, man (99)
hōra, hōrae (f.) - hour (23)
hostis, hostis (m.) - enemy (of the State) (59); (pl., the enemy) (84)

i
iaciō, iacere, iēcī, iactum - I throw (147)
iam - now, already (20)
in - into, against, in, on (19)
inopia, inopiae (f.) - want, lack, need, poverty (23)
īnsula, īnsulae (f.) - island (8)
interim - meanwhile (23)

inveniō, invenīre, invēnī, inventum - I come upon, I find (97)
iter, itineris (n.) - route, journey, march (95); iter faciō - I march (110)
iūdicō, iūdicāre, iūdicāvī, iūdicātum - I judge, I consider (139)

l
labōrō, labōrāre, labōrāvī, labōrātum - I labor, I suffer, I am hard pressed (18)
lapis, lapidis (m.) - stone (145)
laudō, laudāre, laudāvī, laudātum - I praise (9)
lēgātus, lēgātī (m.) - lieutenant, ambassador, envoy (15)
lēx, lēgis (f.) - law (141)
līberō, līberāre, līberāvī, līberātum - I set free, I free (22)
lingua, linguae (f.) - tongue, language (14)
littera, litterae (f.) - letter (of the alphabet); (pl., epistle, letter) (12)
locus, locī (m.) - place, location, situation (21)
lūdus, lūdī (m.) - game, play, school (15)

m
magister, magistrī (m.) - master, teacher, director (143)
male - badly, insufficiently (25)
maneō, manēre, mānsī, mānsum - I stay, I remain (59)
manus, manūs (f.) - hand, band (of men) (93)
mare, maris (n.) - sea (55)

māter, mātris (f.) - mother (61)
memoria, memoriae (f.) - memory (9)
mors, mortis (f.) - death (61)
multitūdō, multitūdinis (f.) - great number, crowd (103)

n
nārrō, nārrāre, nārrāvī, nārrātum - I relate, I tell (16)
nātūra, nātūrae (f.) - nature (11)
nauta, nautae (m.) - sailor (12)
nāvigō, nāvigāre, nāvigāvī, nāvigātum - I sail (10)
nōmen, nōminis (n.) - name (91)
nōn - not (8)
numerus, numerī (m.) - number, group (25)
nunc - now (17)
nūntiō, nūntiāre, nūntiāvī, nūntiātum - I announce, I report (16)
nūntius, nūntī (m.) - messenger, message, news (16)

o
occupō, occupāre, occupāvī, occupātum - I seize, I capture (12)
oppidum, oppidī (n.) - town (139)
oppugnō, oppugnāre, oppugnāvī, oppugnātum - I attack (19)

p
parō, parāre, parāvī, parātum - I prepare, I prepare for (11)
pater, patris (m.) - father (pl., senators) (97)

APPENDIX

Latin - English Glossary

patria, patriae (f.) - country, native land (13)

pecūnia, pecūniae (f.) - wealth, money (24)

poena, poenae (f.) - penalty, punishment (20)

poēta, poētae (m.) - poet (14)

pōnō, pōnere, posuī, positum - I put, I set, I place, I locate (145)

populus, populī (m.) - people, nation, tribe (16)

porta, portae (f.) - gate (9)

portō, portāre, portāvī, portātum - I carry (10)

portus, portūs (m.) - harbor, port (149)

posteā - after that time, afterward, thereafter (23)

potestās, potestātis (f.) - power, opportunity (149)

prōvincia, prōvinciae (f.) - province (15)

puella, puellae (f.) - girl (7)

puer, puerī (m.) - boy (7)

pugnō, pugnāre, pugnāvī, pugnātum - I fight (14)

q

quid - what? (10)

quōmodo - how? (141)

r

rēgina, rēgīnae (f.) - queen (16)

regō, regere, rēxī, rēctum - I rule (149)

reperiō, reperīre, repperī, repertum - I find, I discover (101)

respondeō, respondēre, respondī, respōnsum - I answer, I reply (53)

rēx, rēgis (m.) - king (51)

s

saepe - often (22)

sciō, scīre, scīvī, scītum - I know (95)

scrībō, scrībere, scrīpsī, scrīptum - I write (51)

sed - but (10)

sedeō, sedēre, sēdī, sessum - I sit (61)

semper - always (20)

senātus, senātūs (m.) - senate (103)

servō, servāre, servāvī, servātum - I guard, I save, I keep (20)

servus, servī (m.) - slave (15)

silva, silvae (f.) - forest (7)

socius, socī (m.) - comrade, ally (18)

soror, sorōris (f.) - sister (57)

spectō, spectāre, spectāvī, spectātum - I look at (11)

spēs, speī (f.) - hope (101)

stō, stāre, stetī, stātum - I stand (22)

sunt - they are, there are (8)

superō, superāre, superāvī, superātum - I surpass, I defeat (18)

t

temptō, temptāre, temptāvī, temptātum - I try, I attempt (20)

terra, terrae (f.) - earth, land, country (14)

trādō, trādere, trādidī, trāditum - I hand over, I surrender, I hand down (147)

tuba, tubae (f.) - trumpet (11)

tum - then, at that time (24)

u

ubi - where? (13)

urbs, urbis (f.) - city (57)

v

veniō, venīre, vēnī, ventum - I come (91)

verbum, verbī (n.) - word (49)

vēritās, vēritātis (f.) - truth, trueness (101)

via, viae (f.) - road, way, street (10)

videō, vidēre, vīdī, vīsum - I see (51)

vīlla, vīllae (f.) - farmhouse, country house, villa (12)

vir, virī (m.) - man, husband, hero (49)

vīta, vītae (f.) - life (9)

vocō, vocāre, vocāvī, vocātum - I call (9)

volō, volāre, volāvī, volātum - I fly (21)

vulnerō, vulnerāre, vulnerāvī, vulnerātum - I wound (19)

174

Latin Workbook - Level 4
Copyright © 2000 by Karen Mohs

APPENDIX

English - Latin Glossary

a

accept - accipiō
address - appellō
advice - cōnsilium
after that time - posteā
afterward - posteā
against - in
ally - socius
along with - cum
already - iam
also - et
always - semper
ambassador - lēgātus
and - et
animal - animal
announce - nūntiō
answer - respondeō
anxiety - cūra
approach - adventus
are - sunt
arrival - adventus
assemble - convocō
at - ad
at that time - tum
attack - oppugnō
attempt - temptō
await - exspectō

b

badly - male
band (of men) - manus
behold - ecce
boldness - audācia
boy - puer
bring - dūcō
brother - frāter
but - sed

c

call - vocō, appellō
call together - convocō
captive - captīvus
capture - occupō, capiō
care - dīligentia, cūra
carry - portō
cart - carrus
cause - causa
chance - fortūna
choose - dēligō
city - urbs
clan - gēns
come - veniō
come upon - inveniō
comrade - socius
confidence - fidēs
consider - habeō, iūdicō
country - patria, terra
country house - vīlla
courage - animus (pl.)
crowd - multitūdō

d

daring - audācia
daughter - fīlia
day - diēs
death - mors
declare - cōnfirmō
defeat - superō
diligence - dīligentia
director - magister
discover - reperiō
do - faciō
dwell - habitō

e

earth - terra
encourage - cōnfirmō

enemy (of the State) - hostis
envoy - lēgātus
epistle - littera (pl.), epistula
even - et
exile - fuga

f

faith - fidēs
family - gēns
farmer - agricola
farmhouse - vīlla
father - pater
field - ager, campus
fight - pugnō
find - inveniō, reperiō
flight - fuga
fly - volō
for - ad
for a long time - diū
forces - cōpia (pl.)
foresight - cōnsilium
forest - silva
form (make) a plan - cōnsilium
    capiō
fortune - fortūna
free - līberō
friend - amīcus
friendliness - amīcitia
friendship - amīcitia

g

game - lūdus
gate - porta
gift - dōnum
girl - puella
give - dō
grain - frūmentum
grant - dō
great number - multitūdō

Latin Workbook - Level 4
Copyright © 2000 by Karen Mohs

175

APPENDIX

English - Latin Glossary

group - numerus
guard - servō
guide - dux

h
hand - manus
hand down - trādō
hand over - trādō
harbor - portus
hard pressed - labōrō
have - habeō
hear - audiō
heavens - caelum
hero - vir
hold - habeō
hope - spēs
horse - equus
hour - hōra
how? - quōmodo
human being - homō
husband - vir

i
in - in
insufficiently - male
into - in
is - est
island - īnsula

j
journey - iter
judge - iūdicō

k
keep - servō, habeō
king - rēx
know - sciō

l
labor - labōrō
lack - inopia
land - terra
language - lingua
law - lēx
lead - dūcō
leader - dux
letter - littera, epistula
lieutenant - lēgātus
life - vīta
like - amō
listen to - audiō
live - habitō
location - locus
long - diū
look at - spectō
lord - dominus
love - amō
loyalty - fidēs
luck - fortūna

m
make - faciō; make (form) a plan
     - cōnsilium capiō
man - vir, homō
march - iter, iter faciō
master - dominus, magister
meanwhile - interim
memory - memoria
message - nūntius
messenger - nūntius
mind - animus
money - pecūnia
mother - māter

n
name - appellō, nōmen
nation - populus, gēns

native land - patria
nature - nātūra
near - ad
need - inopia
news - nūntius
not - nōn
now - nunc, iam
number - numerus

o
often - saepe
on - in
opportunity - potestās
owner - dominus

p
penalty - poena
people - populus
place - locus, pōnō
plain - campus
plan - cōnsilium
play - lūdus
please - dēlectō
pledge - fidēs
plenty - cōpia
poet - poēta
point out - dēmōnstrō
port - portus
poverty - inopia
power - potestās
praise - laudō
prepare - parō
prepare for - parō
present - dōnum
prisoner - captīvus
province - prōvincia
punishment - poena
put - pōnō

APPENDIX

English - Latin Glossary

q

queen - rēgīna

r

reason - causa
receive - accipiō
relate - nārrō
remain - maneō
reply - respondeō
report - nūntiō, fāma
reputation - fāma
road - via
route - iter
rule - regō
rumor - fāma

s

sail - nāvigō
sailor - nauta
save - servō
say - dīcō
school - lūdus
sea - mare
see - videō
seize - occupō
senate - senātus
senators - patrēs
set free - līberō
shout - clāmō
show - dēmōnstrō
sister - soror
sit - sedeō
situation - locus
sky - caelum
slave - servus
son - fīlius
spirit - animus
stand - stō
stay - maneō

stone - lapis
story - fābula
street - via
strengthen - cōnfirmō
stroll - ambulō
suffer - labōrō
summon - convocō
supply - cōpia
surpass - superō
surrender - trādō
sword - gladius

t

take - capiō
teacher - magister
tell - nārrō, dīcō
territory - ager
the enemy - hostēs
then - tum, ergō
thereafter - posteā
therefore - ergō
throw - iaciō
to - ad
today - hodiē
tomorrow - crās
tongue - lingua
toward - ad
town - oppidum
tribe - populus
troops - cōpia (pl.)
trueness - vēritās
trumpet - tuba
truth - vēritās
try - temptō

v

villa - vīlla

w

wagon - carrus
wait for - exspectō
walk - ambulō
want - inopia
water - aqua
way - via
wealth - pecūnia
what? - quid
where? - ubi
why? - cūr
wife - fēmina
with - cum
woman - fēmina
word - verbum
wound - vulnerō
write - scrībō

y

year - annus
yesterday - herī

Latin Workbook - Level 4
Copyright © 2000 by Karen Mohs

177

178

Latin Workbook - Level 4
Copyright © 2000 by Karen Mohs

APPENDIX

Latin Alphabet

Capital Letter	Small Letter	Pronunciation	Capital Letter	Small Letter	Pronunciation
Ā	ā	**a** in *father*	N	n	**n** in *nut*
A	a	**a** in *idea*	Ō**	ō**	**o** in *note*
B	b	**b** in *boy*	O**	o**	**o** in *omit*
C	c	**c** in *cat*	P	p	**p** in *pit*
D	d	**d** in *dog*	Q	q	**qu** in *quit*
Ē	ē	**ey** in *obey*	R	r	**r** in *run*
E	e	**e** in *bet*	S	s	**s** in *sit*
F	f	**f** in *fan*	T	t	**t** in *tag*
G	g	**g** in *go*	Ū	ū	**u** in *rule*
H	h	**h** in *hat*	U	u	**u** in *put*
Ī	ī	**i** in *machine*	V	v	**w** in *way*
I*	i*	**i** in *sit*	X	x	**ks** in *socks*
K	k	**k** in *king*	Ȳ	ȳ	form lips to say "oo" but say "ee" instead (held longer)
L	l	**l** in *land*	Y	y	form lips to say "oo" but say "ee" instead (held shorter)
M	m	**m** in *man*	Z	z	**dz** in *adze*

*When functioning as a consonant, **i** has the sound of **y** in *youth*. (See **Special Consonants** below.)
The **ō and the **o** both have a long o sound, but the **ō** is held longer.

Special Sounds

Diphthongs

Letters	Pronunciation
ae	*aye*
au	**ow** in *now*
ei	**ei** in *neighbor*
eu	*ay-oo*
oe	**oy** in *joy*
ui	**uee** in *queen*

Special Consonants

Letters	Pronunciation
bs	*ps*
bt	*pt*
ch	**ch** in *character*
gu	**gu** in *anguish*
i	**y** in *youth*
ph	**ph** in *phone*
su	**su** in *suave*
th	**th** in *thick*

Latin Workbook - Level 4
Copyright © 2000 by Karen Mohs

APPENDIX

Macrons, Syllables, and Accents

I. Rules for Macrons

    1. A vowel **always** has a macron before the letters -ns.

    2. A vowel **never** has a macron before the letters -nt.

    3. When the vowel -e- comes after another vowel, it has a macron.

    4. When an -m, -r, or -t is the last letter in an ending added to a word, the vowel that comes before the -m, -r, or -t is **never** long.

    5. If an -m, -r, or -t is the last letter in a word without an ending, the vowel that comes before the -m, -r, or -t is *almost* **never** long.

II. Rules for Dividing Syllables

    1. When a consonant stands between two vowels or diphthongs, pronounce the consonant in the syllable with the second vowel or diphthong.

    2. When two or more consonants stand between two vowels or diphthongs, pronounce only the last consonant in the syllable with the second vowel or diphthong. (Certain consonants like to stay together, such as h, l, or r coming after c, g, p, b, d, or t.)

    3. When the consonant is a double consonant (x or z)*, place -x- with the vowel before, but -z- with the vowel after.

    4. When the word is compound, separate the prefix from the rest of the word.

III. Rules for Length of Syllables

    1. Syllables which are *long by nature*:

        a. A syllable is long by nature if it contains a long vowel (a vowel with a macron over it).

        b. A syllable is long by nature if it contains a diphthong.

    2. Syllables which are *long by position*:

        a. A syllable is long by position if its vowel is followed by two or more consonants.

        b. A syllable is long by position if its vowel is followed by a double consonant (-x or -z).*

IV. Rules of Accent

    1. On one syllable words, accent the ultima (the only syllable).

    2. On two syllable words, accent the penult.

    3. On three (or more) syllable words, accent the penult if it is long (by nature or by position). Accent the antepenult if the penult is short.

*The letters x and z are called double consonants because two sounds are needed to pronounce them. Pronounce the initial sound with the first syllable and the final sound with the second syllable.

APPENDIX

Principal Parts of the Latin Verb

Latin verbs generally have four main parts, called ***principal parts***.

The Principal Parts of the Verb Amō

amō **Present System**	amāre **Present Infinitive**	amāvī **Perfect System**	amātum **Supine System**
present indicative (active & passive)	*present infinitive* (active & passive)	*perfect indicative* (active)	*perfect indicative* (passive)
imperfect indicative (active & passive)	*imperfect subjunctive* (active & passive)	*pluperfect indicative* (active)	*pluperfect indicative* (passive)
future indicative (active & passive)		*future perfect indicative* (active)	*future perfect indicative* (passive)
present participle (active)		*perfect infinitive* (active)	*perfect infinitive* (passive)
present subjunctive (active & passive)		*perfect subjunctive* (active)	*future infinitive* (active)
future participle (passive)		*pluperfect subjunctive* (active)	*perfect participle* (passive)
			future participle (active)
			perfect subjunctive (passive)
			pluperfect subjunctive (passive)

Word Order

Word order in Latin is not the same as word order in English. In Latin, since the ending determines the role the word plays in the sentence, word order is generally used for emphasis. However, there is a tendency to put the verb last.

Moods of the Latin Verb

Latin verbs are classified according to mood.

The **indicative** *mood* is used to make an assertion or to ask a question.
The **subjunctive** *mood* is used to describe an action that is not real.
The **imperative** *mood* is used to make a command.

A **participle** is a verbal adjective, and an **infinitive** is a verbal noun.

Latin Workbook - Level 4
Copyright © 2000 by Karen Mohs

181

APPENDIX

Voices of the Latin Verb

Voices of the Latin verb:

Active Voice: The subject of the sentence is ***doing an action***.
Example: The man loves the woman.

Passive Voice: The subject of the sentence is ***receiving an action***.
Example: The man is being loved by the woman.

Gender and Case of the Latin Noun

The three genders of Latin nouns are masculine, feminine, and neuter.

Latin nouns are declined using five main *cases*.

The subject of the sentence as well as a noun "linked" to the subject with a linking verb (e.g. *is* or *are*) belong in the **nominative** case. Possession is expressed with the **genitive** case. The indirect object belongs in the **dative** case. The direct object belongs in the **accusative** case. The **ablative** case is used to express special relationships. These cases have other important uses as well.

Special Case Uses

Ablative Case

1. *Ablative of Place Where*
    To indicate location "in" or "on," use the preposition in with the ablative case.

2. *Ablative of Means or Instrument*
    To indicate the means or instrument by which something is done, use the ablative case without a preposition.

3. *Ablative of Manner*
    To indicate the manner in which an action is performed, use the preposition cum with the ablative case.

4. *Ablative of Accompaniment*
    To indicate accompaniment, use the preposition cum with the ablative case.

182

Latin Workbook - Level 4
Copyright © 2000 by Karen Mohs

APPENDIX

First Conjugation

A Latin verb belongs to the first conjugation if its second principal part ends in -āre. Its present tense stem can be found by dropping the -re of the second principal part. The **present tense** is used to describe actions happening in the present time.

Present Active Indicative
(present indicative verb stem + personal ending)

	Singular	Meaning	Plural	Meaning
1st Person	amō	I like (*or* I am liking) (*or* I do like)	amāmus	we like (*or* we are liking) (*or* we do like)
2nd Person	amās	you (s.) like (*or* you are liking) (*or* you do like)	amātis	you (pl.) like (*or* you are liking) (*or* you do like)
3rd Person	amat	he (she, it) likes (*or* he is liking) (*or* he does like)	amant	they like (*or* they are liking) (*or* they do like)

Second Conjugation

A Latin verb belongs to the second conjugation if its second principal part ends in -ēre. Its present tense stem can be found by dropping the -re of the second principal part.

Present Active Indicative
(present indicative verb stem + personal ending)

	Singular	Meaning	Plural	Meaning
1st Person	sedeō	I sit (*or* I am sitting) (*or* I do sit)	sedēmus	we sit (*or* we are sitting) (*or* we do sit)
2nd Person	sedēs	you (s.) sit (*or* you are sitting) (*or* you do sit)	sedētis	you (pl.) sit (*or* you are sitting) (*or* you do sit)
3rd Person	sedet	he (she, it) sits (*or* he is sitting) (*or* he does sit)	sedent	they sit (*or* they are sitting) (*or* they do sit)

Latin Workbook - Level 4
Copyright © 2000 by Karen Mohs

183

APPENDIX

Third Conjugation

A Latin verb belongs to the third conjugation if its second principal part ends in -ere. Its present tense stem can be found by dropping the -ō of the first principal part.

Present Active Indicative
(present indicative verb stem + personal ending)

	Singular	Meaning	Plural	Meaning
1st Person	dīcō	I say (*or* I am saying) (*or* I do say)	dīcimus	we say (*or* we are saying) (*or* we do say)
2nd Person	dīcis	you (s.) say (*or* you are saying) (*or* you do say)	dīcitis	you (pl.) say (*or* you are saying) (*or* you do say)
3rd Person	dīcit	he (she, it) says (*or* he is saying) (*or* he does say)	dīcunt	they say (*or* they are saying) (*or* they do say)

Third I-Stem Conjugation

A Latin verb belongs to the third i-stem conjugation if its second principal part ends in -ere and its present tense stem ends in -i. Its present tense stem can be found by dropping the -ō of the first principal part.

Present Active Indicative
(present indicative verb stem + personal ending)

	Singular	Meaning	Plural	Meaning
1st Person	capiō	I take (*or* I am taking) (*or* I do take)	capimus	we take (*or* we are taking) (*or* we do take)
2nd Person	capis	you (s.) take (*or* you are taking) (*or* you do take)	capitis	you (pl.) take (*or* you are taking) (*or* you do take)
3rd Person	capit	he (she, it) takes (*or* he is taking) (*or* he does take)	capiunt	they take (*or* they are taking) (*or* they do take)

184

Latin Workbook - Level 4
Copyright © 2000 by Karen Mohs

APPENDIX

Fourth Conjugation

A Latin verb belongs to the fourth conjugation if its second principal part ends in -īre. Its present tense stem can be found by dropping the -re of the second principal part.

Present Active Indicative
(present indicative verb stem + personal ending)

	Singular	Meaning	Plural	Meaning
1st Person	audiō	I hear (*or* I am hearing) (*or* I do hear)	audīmus	we hear (*or* we are hearing) (*or* we do hear)
2nd Person	audīs	you (s.) hear (*or* you are hearing) (*or* you do hear)	audītis	you (pl.) hear (*or* you are hearing) (*or* you do hear)
3rd Person	audit	he (she, it) hears (*or* he is hearing) (*or* he does hear)	audiunt	they hear (*or* they are hearing) (*or* they do hear)

The "Being" Verb

The Latin "being" verb is used to "link" a subject (**nominative** case) with another word in the **nominative** case that renames the subject (*predicate nominative*).

Present Indicative

	Singular	Meaning	Plural	Meaning
1st Person	sum	I am	sumus	we are
2nd Person	es	you (s.) are	estis	you (pl.) are
3rd Person	est	he (she, it) is, there is	sunt	they are, there are

Latin Workbook - Level 4
Copyright © 2000 by Karen Mohs

185

APPENDIX

First Declension

A Latin noun belongs to the first declension if the genitive singular ends in -ae. Remove the -ae from the genitive singular to find the stem. These nouns are usually feminine, unless they describe males in Latin culture such as sailors, poets, or farmers.

	Singular	*Meaning*	*Plural*	*Meaning*
Nominative	puella	a girl (*or* the girl)	puellae	girls (*or* the girls)
Genitive	puellae	of a girl (*or* of the girl)	puellārum	of girls (*or* of the girls)
Dative	puellae	to/for a girl (*or* to/for the girl)	puellīs	to/for girls (*or* to/for the girls)
Accusative	puellam	a girl (*or* the girl)	puellās	girls (*or* the girls)
Ablative	puellā	by/with* a girl (*or* by/with* the girl)	puellīs	by/with* girls (*or* by/with* the girls)

*The translations given above are just a sampling of the many possible meanings of the ablative case.

Second Declension

A Latin noun belongs to the second declension if the genitive singular ends in -ī. Remove the -ī from the genitive singular to find the stem. If a second declension nominative ends in -us, it is usually masculine.

	Singular	*Meaning*	*Plural*	*Meaning*
Nominative	amīcus	a friend (*or* the friend)	amīcī	friends (*or* the friends)
Genitive	amīcī	of a friend (*or* of the friend)	amīcōrum	of friends (*or* of the friends)
Dative	amīcō	to/for a friend (*or* to/for the friend)	amīcīs	to/for friends (*or* to/for the friends)
Accusative	amīcum	a friend (*or* the friend)	amīcōs	friends (*or* the friends)
Ablative	amīcō	by/with* a friend (*or* by/with* the friend)	amīcīs	by/with* friends (*or* by/with* the friends)

*The translations given above are just a sampling of the many possible meanings of the ablative case.

APPENDIX

Second Declension -ius

A Latin second declension -ius noun is declined like a second declension -us noun except in the genitive singular. The expected genitive singular -iī of these -ius nouns is shortened to -ī. However, the stem retains the -i- [soci-].

	Singular	*Meaning*	*Plural*	*Meaning*
Nominative	socius	an ally (*or* the ally)	sociī	allies (*or* the allies)
Genitive	socī	of an ally (*or* of the ally)	sociōrum	of allies (*or* of the allies)
Dative	sociō	to/for an ally (*or* to/for the ally)	sociīs	to/for allies (*or* to/for the allies)
Accusative	socium	an ally (*or* the ally)	sociōs	allies (*or* the allies)
Ablative	sociō	by/with* an ally (*or* by/with* the ally)	sociīs	by/with* allies (*or* by/with* the allies)

*The translations given above are just a sampling of the many possible meanings of the ablative case.

Second Declension -er
(as in puer)

A Latin noun belongs to the second declension if the genitive singular ends in -ī. Remove the -ī from the genitive singular to find the stem. If a second declension nominative ends in -er, it is usually masculine.

	Singular	*Meaning*	*Plural*	*Meaning*
Nominative	puer	a boy (*or* the boy)	puerī	boys (*or* the boys)
Genitive	puerī	of a boy (*or* of the boy)	puerōrum	of boys (*or* of the boys)
Dative	puerō	to/for a boy (*or* to/for the boy)	puerīs	to/for boys (*or* to/for the boys)
Accusative	puerum	a boy (*or* the boy)	puerōs	boys (*or* the boys)
Ablative	puerō	by/with* a boy (*or* by/with* the boy)	puerīs	by/with* boys (*or* by/with* the boys)

*The translations given above are just a sampling of the many possible meanings of the ablative case.

Latin Workbook - Level 4
Copyright © 2000 by Karen Mohs

APPENDIX

Second Declension -er
(as in ager)

A Latin noun belongs to the second declension if the genitive singular ends in -ī. Remove the -ī from the genitive singular to find the stem. If a second declension nominative ends in -er, it is usually masculine.

	Singular	Meaning	Plural	Meaning
Nominative	ager	a field (*or* the field)	agrī	fields (*or* the fields)
Genitive	agrī	of a field (*or* of the field)	agrōrum	of fields (*or* of the fields)
Dative	agrō	to/for a field (*or* to/for the field)	agrīs	to/for fields (*or* to/for the fields)
Accusative	agrum	a field (*or* the field)	agrōs	fields (*or* the fields)
Ablative	agrō	by/with* a field (*or* by/with* the field)	agrīs	by/with* fields (*or* by/with* the fields)

*The translations given above are just a sampling of the many possible meanings of the ablative case.

Second Declension Neuter

A Latin noun belongs to the second declension if the genitive singular ends in -ī. Remove the -ī from the genitive singular to find the stem. If a second declension nominative ends in -um, it is neuter.

	Singular	Meaning	Plural	Meaning
Nominative	caelum	a sky (*or* the sky)	caela	skies (*or* the skies)
Genitive	caelī	of a sky (*or* of the sky)	caelōrum	of skies (*or* of the skies)
Dative	caelō	to/for a sky (*or* to/for the sky)	caelīs	to/for skies (*or* to/for the skies)
Accusative	caelum	a sky (*or* the sky)	caela	skies (*or* the skies)
Ablative	caelō	by/with* a sky (*or* by/with* the sky)	caelīs	by/with* skies (*or* by/with* the skies)

*The translations given above are just a sampling of the many possible meanings of the ablative case.

APPENDIX

Third Declension
(as in frāter)

A Latin noun belongs to the third declension if the genitive singular ends in -is. Remove the -is from the genitive singular to find the stem.

	Singular	*Meaning*	*Plural*	*Meaning*
Nominative	frāter	a brother (*or* the brother)	frātrēs	brothers (*or* the brothers)
Genitive	frātris	of a brother (*or* of the brother)	frātrum	of brothers (*or* of the brothers)
Dative	frātrī	to/for a brother (*or* to/for the brother)	frātribus	to/for brothers (*or* to/for the brothers)
Accusative	frātrem	a brother (*or* the brother)	frātrēs	brothers (*or* the brothers)
Ablative	frātre	by/with* a brother (*or* by/with* the brother)	frātribus	by/with* brothers (*or* by/with* the brothers)

*The translations given above are just a sampling of the many possible meanings of the ablative case.

Third Declension
(as in soror)

A Latin noun belongs to the third declension if the genitive singular ends in -is. Remove the -is from the genitive singular to find the stem.

	Singular	*Meaning*	*Plural*	*Meaning*
Nominative	soror	a sister (*or* the sister)	sorōrēs	sisters (*or* the sisters)
Genitive	sorōris	of a sister (*or* of the sister)	sorōrum	of sisters (*or* of the sisters)
Dative	sorōrī	to/for a sister (*or* to/for the sister)	sorōribus	to/for sisters (*or* to/for the sisters)
Accusative	sorōrem	a sister (*or* the sister)	sorōrēs	sisters (*or* the sisters)
Ablative	sorōre	by/with* a sister (*or* by/with* the sister)	sorōribus	by/with* sisters (*or* by/with* the sisters)

*The translations given above are just a sampling of the many possible meanings of the ablative case.

Latin Workbook - Level 4
Copyright © 2000 by Karen Mohs

APPENDIX

Third Declension I-Stem

A Latin noun belongs to the third declension if the genitive singular ends in -is. Remove the -is from the genitive singular to find the stem. Certain third declension nouns require an -ium (rather than -um) ending in the genitive plural. These "third declension i-stems" include the following:

1. a masculine or feminine noun that ends in -ēs or -is in the nominative singular and has the same number of syllables in the **nominative** and **genitive** singular cases (e.g. hostis)
2. a masculine or feminine noun that ends in -ns or -rs (e.g. gēns)
3. a masculine or feminine noun that has only one syllable in the nominative singular and its stem ends in two consonants (e.g. urbs)
4. a neuter noun that ends in -al or -e in the nominative singular (e.g. mare)

Notice the -ī in the ablative singular and the -ia in the nominative and accusative plural of **neuter** third declension i-stems.

Singular

Nominative	hostis	gēns	urbs	mare
Genitive	hostis	gentis	urbis	maris
Dative	hostī	gentī	urbī	marī
Accusative	hostem	gentem	urbem	mare
Ablative	hoste	gente	urbe	marī

Plural

Nominative	hostēs	gentēs	urbēs	maria
Genitive	hostium	gentium	urbium	marium
Dative	hostibus	gentibus	urbibus	maribus
Accusative	hostēs	gentēs	urbēs	maria
Ablative	hostibus	gentibus	urbibus	maribus

APPENDIX

Third Declension Neuter

A Latin noun belongs to the third declension if the genitive singular ends in -is. Remove the -is from the genitive singular to find the stem. Neuter nouns have the same ending in the nominative and accusative cases. Plural nominative and accusative neuter nouns always end in -a.

	Singular	*Meaning*	*Plural*	*Meaning*
Nominative	nōmen	a name (*or* the name)	nōmina	names (*or* the names)
Genitive	nōminis	of a name (*or* of the name)	nōminum	of names (*or* of the names)
Dative	nōminī	to/for a name (*or* to/for the name)	nōminibus	to/for names (*or* to/for the names)
Accusative	nōmen	a name (*or* the name)	nōmina	names (*or* the names)
Ablative	nōmine	by/with* a name (*or* by/with* the name)	nōminibus	by/with* names (*or* by/with* the names)

*The translations given above are just a sampling of the many possible meanings of the ablative case.

Fourth Declension

A Latin noun belongs to the fourth declension if the genitive singular ends in -ūs. Remove the -ūs from the genitive singular to find the stem. These nouns are usually masculine. However, manus is feminine.

	Singular	*Meaning*	*Plural*	*Meaning*
Nominative	manus	a hand (*or* the hand)	manūs	hands (*or* the hands)
Genitive	manūs	of a hand (*or* of the hand)	manuum	of hands (*or* of the hands)
Dative	manuī	to/for a hand (*or* to/for the hand)	manibus	to/for hands (*or* to/for the hands)
Accusative	manum	a hand (*or* the hand)	manūs	hands (*or* the hands)
Ablative	manū	by/with* a hand (*or* by/with* the hand)	manibus	by/with* hands (*or* by/with* the hands)

*The translations given above are just a sampling of the many possible meanings of the ablative case.

Latin Workbook - Level 4
Copyright © 2000 by Karen Mohs

APPENDIX

Fifth Declension
(as in diēs)

A Latin noun belongs to the fifth declension if the genitive singular ends in -ēī or -eī. Remove the ending from the genitive singular to find the stem. (The fifth declension ending is actually -ī. The -ē- [or -e- if after a consonant and before a vowel] is the stem ending. However, it is easy to recognize this declension by the -ēī or -eī of the genitive singular.)

	Singular	Meaning	Plural	Meaning
Nominative	diēs	a day (*or* the day)	diēs	days (*or* the days)
Genitive	diēī	of a day (*or* of the day)	diērum	of days (*or* of the days)
Dative	diēī	to/for a day (*or* to/for the day)	diēbus	to/for days (*or* to/for the days)
Accusative	diem	a day (*or* the day)	diēs	days (*or* the days)
Ablative	diē	by/with* a day (*or* by/with* the day)	diēbus	by/with* days (*or* by/with* the days)

*The translations given above are just a sampling of the many possible meanings of the ablative case.

Fifth Declension
(as in spēs)

	Singular	Meaning	Plural	Meaning
Nominative	spēs	a hope (*or* the hope)	spēs	hopes (*or* the hopes)
Genitive	speī	of a hope (*or* of the hope)	spērum	of hopes (*or* of the hopes)
Dative	speī	to/for a hope (*or* to/for the hope)	spēbus	to/for hopes (*or* to/for the hopes)
Accusative	spem	a hope (*or* the hope)	spēs	hopes (*or* the hopes)
Ablative	spē	by/with* a hope (*or* by/with* the hope)	spēbus	by/with* hopes (*or* by/with* the hopes)

*The translations given above are just a sampling of the many possible meanings of the ablative case.

APPENDIX

Index

ablative case, 35-37, 69; See appendix pages 182, 186-192.

*ablative of **accompaniment***, 69; See appendix page 182.

*ablative of **manner***, 37; See appendix page 182.

*ablative of **means or instrument***, 36; See appendix page 182.

*ablative of **place where***, 35; See appendix page 182.

accent rules, 47; See appendix page 180.

accompaniment, 69; See appendix page 182.

accusative case, 29; See appendix pages 182, 186-192.

alphabet, 1-3; See appendix page 179.

antepenult, 43, 47; See appendix page 180.

"being" verb, 67; See appendix page 185.

"by means of ", 36.

case ending, See *nominative case, genitive case,* etc.

compound words, syllable division of, 44; See appendix page 180.

conjugation, See *first conjugation, second conjugation,* etc.

connective -que, 68.

cōnsilium + capiō, 121.

consonants, special sounds, 4; in syllable division, 44; in syllable length, 45; See appendix pages 179, 180.

cum, to show ***manner***, 37; to show ***accompaniment***, 69; See appendix page 182.

dative case, 34; See appendix pages 182, 186-192.

declension, 71; See *first declension, second declension,* etc.

diphthongs, 3; in syllable division, 44; in syllable length, 45; See appendix pages 179, 180.

direct object of sentence, 29; See appendix page 182.

double consonant, in syllable division, 44; in syllable length, 45; See appendix page 180.

-er second declension noun, 73; See appendix pages 187-188.

feminine gender, 7, 49, 71, 79-80; See appendix page 182.

fifth declension, 131; See appendix page 192.

first conjugation, 27, 39, 83; See appendix page 183.

first declension, 29-31, 34-37, 71; masculine forms, 71; See appendix page 186.

flashcard tips, how to learn nouns, 7, 49; how to learn verbs, 9, 51; See appendix page 195.

fourth conjugation, 127; See appendix page 185.

fourth declension, 123; See appendix page 191.

gender, 7, 49, 71-72, 79-81; See appendix page 182.

genitive case, 30, 71, 75, 79, 123, 131; See appendix pages 182, 186-192.

hostis, requires plural in Latin for more than one, 84.

i-stem noun, masculine and feminine, 79-80; neuter, 81; See appendix page 190.

i-stem verb, 119; See appendix page 184.

"in", 36; See appendix page 182.

in, *to show **place where***, 35; See appendix page 182.

indicative, present active, 27, 83, 87, 119, 127; See appendix pages 181, 183-185.

indirect object of sentence, 34; See appendix page 182.

iter + faciō, 110.

-ius second declension noun, 29-31, 34, 73; See appendix page 187.

letter pronunciation, 1-3; See appendix page 179.

"linking" subject to predicate nominative, 33, 67; See appendix pages 182, 185.

long by nature, 45; See appendix page 180.

long by position, 45; See appendix page 180.

macron, rules for use, 41; See appendix page 180.

manner, 37; See appendix page 182.

masculine gender, 7, 49, 71, 79-80; See appendix page 182.

APPENDIX

Index

means or instrument, 36; See appendix page 182.

-ne, 68, 113.

neuter gender, 7, 49, 71-72, 81, 109; See appendix page 182.

no question, 113.

nominative case, 31, 67, 71, 79; See appendix pages 182, 186-192.

nōnne, 113.

noun, 29-31, 34-37, 69, 71-73, 75, 79-81, 109, 123, 131; See appendix pages 182, 186-192.

num, 113.

number expressed, by ending on verb, 27, 67, 83, 87, 119, 127; by ending on noun, 29-31, 34-36, 69, 72-73, 75, 79-81, 109, 123, 131; See appendix pages 183-192.

"*o*" *sounds*, 2; See appendix page 179.

"*on*", 36; See appendix page 182.

penult, 43, 47; See appendix page 180.

place where, 35; See appendix page 182.

populus, singular and plural meanings, 16.

possession, 30, 71; See appendix page 182.

predicate nominative, 67.

present stem, 39, 83, 87, 119, 127; See appendix pages 183-185.

present tense, 27, 67, 83, 87, 119, 127; See appendix pages 181, 183-185.

principal parts, 39, 83, 87, 119, 127; of sum, 39; See appendix page 181.

pronunciation, alphabet, 1-3; diphthongs, 3; special consonant sounds, 4; See appendix page 179.

-que, 68.

question sentence, *yes* or *no*, 68, 113; expects *yes*, 113; expects *no*, 113.

same spelling for different uses, 31, 34-35.

second conjugation, 83; See appendix page 183.

second declension, masculine, 29-31, 34-36, 69, 71, 73; neuter, 72; See appendix pages 186-188.

sentence, direct object of, 29; indirect object of, 34; possession, 30; subject of, 31; See appendix page 182.

special case uses, 35-37, 69; See appendix page 182.

special consonant sounds, 4; See appendix page 179.

stem, of verb, 39, 83, 87, 119, 127; of noun, 73; See appendix pages 183-192.

subject of sentence, 31, 67, 71; See appendix page 182.

sum, principal parts of, 39.

syllable, names of, 43; rules of division, 44; length of, 45; See appendix page 180.

third conjugation, 87; i-stem, 119; See appendix page 184.

third declension, masculine and feminine, 75; neuter, 109; masculine and feminine i-stem, 79-80; neuter i-stem, 81; See appendix pages 189-191.

ultima, 43, 47; See appendix page 180.

verb, 27, 67, 83, 87, 119, 127; principal parts, 39; verb last in sentence, 33; See appendix pages 181-185.

vowels, 1-3; in syllable division, 44, in syllable length, 45; See appendix pages 179, 180.

"*where*", 35; See appendix page 182.

"*with*", 36, 37, 69.

word order, 33; See appendix page 181.

yes or *no question*, 68, 113.

yes question, 113.

194

Latin Workbook - Level 4
Copyright © 2000 by Karen Mohs

APPENDIX

Flashcard Tips

1. Remember to practice flashcards daily.

2. Do not move ahead in the workbook if your student is struggling for mastery. Review the flashcards every day until your student is confident and ready to learn more.

3. For each noun, your student must now learn both the nominative and the genitive forms, as well as the gender. (See page 7.) As cards are flashed, ask your student to note the ending on the genitive form. Ask him to identify the declension based on the genitive ending. For example, if the genitive form ends in -ae, the noun belongs to the first declension. If it ends in -ī, the noun belongs to the second declension. All five declensions are taught in this workbook.

4. For each verb, your student must learn all four principal parts. (See page 9.) As cards are flashed, ask your student to note the ending on the second principal part. Ask him to identify the conjugation based on that ending. For example, if the second principal part ends in -āre, the verb belongs to the first conjugation. The present active indicative of all four conjugations are taught in this workbook.

5. Your student should thoroughly learn each conjugation and declension card. This will require extra effort, but will greatly enhance your student's understanding. Please help your student apply the endings on these cards to all appropriate vocabulary words.

6. When the number of the cards becomes too cumbersome to review in one day, remove the cards the student knows without hesitation and put them in an "Occasional Practice" stack. Review the "Occasional Practice" stack once a week.

Latin Workbook - Level 4
Copyright © 2000 by Karen Mohs

Latin Workbook - Level 4
Copyright © 2000 by Karen Mohs

"Latin's Not So Tough!"
Level Four
Feedback Form

Dear Friend of Greek 'n' Stuff:

Please use the following form to give us your feedback regarding this workbook. Mail your comments to:

> Greek 'n' Stuff
> P.O. Box 882
> Moline, IL 61266-0882

If you prefer, you may send your comments via fax (309-796-2706).

What did you enjoy about this book?

_____

_____

_____

_____

In what ways could this book be more effective?

_____

_____

_____

_____

Circle "yes" beside the Learning Aids which you found helpful in your studies. We would also like to know what you especially liked about each (and/or any suggestions you may have for improvement).

yes   "Answers Only" key _____

yes   "Full Text" key _____

yes   Quizzes/Exams _____

yes   "Flashcards on a Ring" _____

yes   Pronunciation CD/tape _____

yes   Greek 'n' Stuff's Internet homepage (**www.greeknstuff.com**) with its "Greek and Latin Words of the Month" _____

(front)	(back)
puella	(Start on page 7.) (Level 4) puellae (f.) girl
fēmina	(Page 7) (Level 4) fēminae (f.) woman, wife
puer	(Page 7) (Level 4) puerī (m.) boy
silva	(Page 7) (Level 4) silvae (f.) forest
agricola	(Page 7) (Level 4) agricolae (m.) farmer
aqua	(Page 7) (Level 4) aquae (f.) water

(front)	(back)
est	(Page 8) (Level 4) he is, she is, it is, there is
nōn	(Page 8) (Level 4) not
et	(Page 8) (Level 4) and, also, even
ad	(Page 8) (Level 4) to, near, toward, for, at
īnsula	(Page 8) (Level 4) īnsulae (f.) island
sunt	(Page 8) (Level 4) they are, there are

(front)	(back)
laudō	(Page 9) (Level 4) laudāre laudāvī laudātum I praise
vocō	(Page 9) (Level 4) vocāre vocāvī vocātum I call
dō	(Page 9) (Level 4) dare dedī datum I give, I grant
vīta	(Page 9) (Level 4) vītae (f.) life
porta	(Page 9) (Level 4) portae (f.) gate
memoria	(Page 9) (Level 4) memoriae (f.) memory

(front)	(back)
nāvigō	(Page 10) (Level 4) nāvigāre nāvigāvī nāvigātum I sail
sed	(Page 10) (Level 4) but
fortūna	(Page 10) (Level 4) fortūnae (f.) fortune, chance, luck
via	(Page 10) (Level 4) viae (f.) road, way, street
portō	(Page 10) (Level 4) portāre portāvī portātum I carry
quid	(Page 10) (Level 4) what?

(front)	(back)
tuba	(Page 11) (Level 4) tubae (f.) trumpet
ager	(Page 11) (Level 4) agrī (m.) field, territory
parō	(Page 11) (Level 4) parāre parāvī parātum I prepare, I prepare for
amīcus	(Page 11) (Level 4) amīcī (m.) friend
spectō	(Page 11) (Level 4) spectāre spectāvī spectātum I look at
nātūra	(Page 11) (Level 4) nātūrae (f.) nature

(front)	(back)
campus	(Page 12)　　　　　　　　(Level 4) campī (m.) field, plain
occupō	(Page 12)　　　　　　　　(Level 4) occupāre occupāvī occupātum I seize, I capture
cum	(Page 12)　　　　　　　　(Level 4) along with, with
nauta	(Page 12)　　　　　　　　(Level 4) nautae (m.) sailor
vīlla	(Page 12)　　　　　　　　(Level 4) vīllae (f.) farmhouse, country house, villa
littera	(Page 12)　　　　　　　　(Level 4) litterae (f.) letter (of the alphabet), (if plural: epistle, letter)

(front)	(back)
ubi	(Page 13) (Level 4) where?
filius	(Page 13) (Level 4) filī (m.) son
patria	(Page 13) (Level 4) patriae (f.) country, native land
filia	(Page 13) (Level 4) filiae (f.) daughter
amīcitia	(Page 13) (Level 4) amīcitiae (f.) friendliness, friendship
amō	(Page 13) (Level 4) amāre amāvī amātum I love, I like

(front)	(back)
lingua	(Page 14) (Level 4) linguae (f.) tongue, language
equus	(Page 14) (Level 4) equī (m.) horse
poēta	(Page 14) (Level 4) poētae (m.) poet
annus	(Page 14) (Level 4) annī (m.) year
pugnō	(Page 14) (Level 4) pugnāre pugnāvī pugnātum I fight
terra	(Page 14) (Level 4) terrae (f.) earth, land, country

(front)	(back)
gladius	(Page 15) (Level 4) gladī (m.) sword
prōvincia	(Page 15) (Level 4) prōvinciae (f.) province
lēgātus	(Page 15) (Level 4) lēgātī (m.) lieutenant, envoy, ambassador
lūdus	(Page 15) (Level 4) lūdī (m.) game, play, school
appellō	(Page 15) (Level 4) appellāre appellāvī appellātum I address, I call, I name
servus	(Page 15) (Level 4) servī (m.) slave

(front)	(back)
nūntius	(Page 16)　　　　　　　　(Level 4) nūntī (m.) messenger, message, news
nūntiō	(Page 16)　　　　　　　　(Level 4) nūntiāre nūntiāvī nūntiātum I announce, I report
nārrō	(Page 16)　　　　　　　　(Level 4) nārrāre nārrāvī nārrātum I relate, I tell
fāma	(Page 16)　　　　　　　　(Level 4) fāmae (f.) report, rumor, reputation
populus	(Page 16)　　　　　　　　(Level 4) populī (m.) people, nation, tribe
rēgīna	(Page 16)　　　　　　　　(Level 4) rēgīnae (f.) queen

(front)	(back)
exspectō	(Page 17) (Level 4) exspectāre exspectāvī exspectātum I await, I wait for
epistula	(Page 17) (Level 4) epistulae (f.) letter, epistle
habitō	(Page 17) (Level 4) habitāre habitāvī habitātum I live, I dwell
nunc	(Page 17) (Level 4) now
fābula	(Page 17) (Level 4) fābulae (f.) story
dēlectō	(Page 17) (Level 4) dēlectāre dēlectāvī dēlectātum I please

(front)	(back)
labōrō	(Page 18) (Level 4) labōrāre labōrāvī labōrātum I labor, I suffer, I am hard pressed
causa	(Page 18) (Level 4) causae (f.) cause, reason
socius	(Page 18) (Level 4) socī (m.) comrade, ally
dīligentia	(Page 18) (Level 4) dīligentiae (f.) diligence, care
convocō	(Page 18) (Level 4) convocāre convocāvī convocātum I call together, I assemble, I summon
superō	(Page 18) (Level 4) superāre superāvī superātum I surpass, I defeat

(front)	(back)
cōpia	(Page 19) (Level 4) cōpiae (f.) plenty, supply (if plural: troops, forces)
in	(Page 19) (Level 4) into, against, in, on
oppugnō	(Page 19) (Level 4) oppugnāre oppugnāvī oppugnātum I attack
diū	(Page 19) (Level 4) for a long time, long
vulnerō	(Page 19) (Level 4) vulnerāre vulnerāvī vulnerātum I wound
fuga	(Page 19) (Level 4) fugae (f.) flight, exile

(front)	(back)
iam	(Page 20) (Level 4) now, already
temptō	(Page 20) (Level 4) temptāre temptāvī temptātum I try, I attempt
herī	(Page 20) (Level 4) yesterday
servō	(Page 20) (Level 4) servāre servāvī servātum I guard, I save, I keep
poena	(Page 20) (Level 4) poenae (f.) penalty, punishment
semper	(Page 20) (Level 4) always

(front)	(back)
captīvus	(Page 21) (Level 4) captīvī (m.) captive, prisoner
locus	(Page 21) (Level 4) locī (m.) place, location, situation
audācia	(Page 21) (Level 4) audāciae (f.) boldness, daring
hodiē	(Page 21) (Level 4) today
volō	(Page 21) (Level 4) volāre volāvī volātum I fly
animus	(Page 21) (Level 4) animī (m.) mind, spirit (if plural: courage)

(front)	(back)
crās	(Page 22) (Level 4) tomorrow
carrus	(Page 22) (Level 4) carrī (m.) cart, wagon
cūra	(Page 22) (Level 4) cūrae (f.) care, anxiety
stō	(Page 22) (Level 4) stāre stetī stātum I stand
saepe	(Page 22) (Level 4) often
līberō	(Page 22) (Level 4) līberāre līberāvī līberātum I set free, I free

(front)	(back)
interim	(Page 23) (Level 4) meanwhile
cūr	(Page 23) (Level 4) why?
dēmōnstrō	(Page 23) (Level 4) dēmōnstrāre dēmōnstrāvī dēmōnstrātum I point out, I show
hōra	(Page 23) (Level 4) hōrae (f.) hour
posteā	(Page 23) (Level 4) after that time, afterward, thereafter
inopia	(Page 23) (Level 4) inopiae (f.) want, lack, need, poverty

(front)	(back)
pecūnia	(Page 24) (Level 4) pecūniae (f.) wealth, money
cōnfīrmō	(Page 24) (Level 4) cōnfirmāre cōnfirmāvī cōnfirmātum I strengthen, I encourage, I declare
tum	(Page 24) (Level 4) then, at that time
clāmō	(Page 24) (Level 4) clāmāre clāmāvī clāmātum I shout
dominus	(Page 24) (Level 4) dominī (m.) master, lord, owner
ambulō	(Page 24) (Level 4) ambulāre ambulāvī ambulātum I stroll, I walk

(front)	(back)
male	(Page 25) — (Level 4) badly, insufficiently
numerus	(Page 25) — (Level 4) numerī (m.) number, group
first conjugation present active indicative	(Page 27) — (Level 4) amō — I like — amāmus — we like amās — you (sing.) like — amātis — you (pl.) like amat — he (she, it) likes — amant — they like
first declension (singular)	(Page 37) — (Level 4) cūra — the care cūrae — of the care cūrae — to (or for) the care cūram — the care cum cūrā — with care
first declension (plural)	(Page 37) — (Level 4) cūrae — the cares cūrārum — of the cares cūrīs — to (or for) the cares cūrās — the cares cum cūrīs — with cares
second declension (singular)	(Page 37) — (Level 4) lūdus — the school lūdī — of the school lūdō — to (or for) the school lūdum — the school in lūdō — in the school

(front)	(back)
second declension (plural)	(Page 37) (Level 4) lūdī — the schools lūdōrum — of the schools lūdīs — to (or for) the schools lūdōs — the schools in lūdīs — in the schools
second declension -ius (singular)	(Page 37) (Level 4) gladius — the sword gladī — of the sword gladiō — to (or for) the sword gladium — the sword gladiō — with the sword
second declension -ius (plural)	(Page 37) (Level 4) gladiī — the swords gladiōrum — of the swords gladiīs — to (or for) the swords gladiōs — the swords gladiīs — with the swords
principal parts of amō	(Page 39) (Level 4) **amō amāre amāvī amātum**
A vowel always has a macron before what letters?	(Page 41) (Level 4) **-ns**
A vowel never has a macron before what letters?	(Page 41) (Level 4) **-nt**

(front)	(back)
In most fifth declension words, when the vowel -e- comes after another vowel, does it have a macron?	(Page 41) (Level 4) **yes**
What three letters, if **last** in a word, usually keep the vowel before that final letter short?	(Page 41) (Level 4) **m r t**
Syllables: e pis tu la 3 2 1	(Page 43) (Level 4) 1. ultima 2. penult 3. antepenult
A Latin word has as many syllables as it has what?	(Page 44) (Level 4) vowels or diphthongs
Correctly pronounce these Latin words: populus fābula rēgīnae causae	(Page 44) (Level 4) po' pu lus fā' bu la rē gī' nae cau' sae
Correctly pronounce these Latin words: temptō fortūna captīvus annus	(Page 44) (Level 4) temp' tō for tū' na cap tī' vus an' nus

(front)	(back)
Correctly pronounce these Latin words: patria amplus agricola acclāmō	(Page 44) (Level 4) pa' tri a am' plus a gri' co la ac clā' mō
Correctly pronounce these Latin words: uxor gāza saxum citharizō	(Page 44) (Level 4) ux' or gā' za sax' um ci tha' ri zō
Correctly pronounce these Latin words: exspectō subtimeō convocō indūcō	(Page 44) (Level 4) ex spec' tō sub ti' me ō con' vo cō in dū' cō
When is a syllable long by **nature**?	(Page 45) (Level 4) when it contains a long vowel or a diphthong
When is a syllable long by **position**?	(Page 45) (Level 4) when its vowel is followed by two or more consonants or by a double consonant (X or Z)
On words having two syllables, which syllable is accented?	(Page 47) (Level 4) the penult

(front)	(back)
On words having three syllables and having a long penult, which syllable is accented?	(Page 47) (Level 4) the penult
On words having three syllables and having a short penult, which syllable is accented?	(Page 47) (Level 4) the antepenult
verbum	(Page 49) (Level 4) verbī (n.) word
vir	(Page 49) (Level 4) virī (m.) man, husband, hero
caelum	(Page 49) (Level 4) caelī (n.) sky, heavens
rēx	(Page 51) (Level 4) rēgis (m.) king

(front)	(back)
videō	(Page 51) (Level 4) vidēre vīdī vīsum I see
scrībō	(Page 51) (Level 4) scrībere scrīpsī scrīptum I write
gēns	(Page 53) (Level 4) gentis (f.) nation, family, clan
dīcō	(Page 53) (Level 4) dīcere dīxī dictum I say, I tell
respondeō	(Page 53) (Level 4) respondēre respondī respōnsum I answer, I reply
mare	(Page 55) (Level 4) maris (n.) sea

(front)	(back)
frāter	(Page 55) (Level 4) frātris (m.) brother
dūcō	(Page 55) (Level 4) dūcere dūxī ductum I lead, I bring
urbs	(Page 57) (Level 4) urbis (f.) city
frūmentum	(Page 57) (Level 4) frūmentī (n.) grain
soror	(Page 57) (Level 4) sorōris (f.) sister
hostis	(Page 59) (Level 4) hostis (m.) enemy (of the State)

(front)	(back)
maneō	(Page 59) (Level 4) manēre mānsī mānsum I stay, I remain
dēligō	(Page 59) (Level 4) dēligere dēlēgī dēlēctum I choose
māter	(Page 61) (Level 4) mātris (f.) mother
sedeō	(Page 61) (Level 4) sedēre sēdī sessum I sit
mors	(Page 61) (Level 4) mortis (f.) death
the being verb present indicative	(Page 67) (Level 4)

For the last card:

sum	I am	sumus	we are
es	you (sing.) are	estis	you (pl.) are
est	he (she, it) is, there is	sunt	they are, there are

(front)	(back)
Nouns that end with -ae in the genitive singular belong to which declension?	(Page 71) (Level 4) the first declension
Nouns that end with -ī in the genitive singular belong to which declension?	(Page 71) (Level 4) the second declension
second declension neuter (singular)	(Page 72) (Level 4) caelum — the sky caelī — of the sky caelō — to (or for) the sky caelum — the sky in caelō — in the sky
second declension neuter (plural)	(Page 72) (Level 4) caela — the skies caelōrum — of the skies caelīs — to (or for) the skies caela — the skies in caelīs — in the skies
How do you find the stem of a noun?	(Page 73) (Level 4) remove the genitive singular ending
second declension -er (singular) as in puer	(Page 73) (Level 4) puer — the boy puerī — of the boy puerō — to (or for) the boy puerum — the boy cum puerō — with the boy

(front)	(back)
second declension -er (plural) as in **puer**	(Page 73) (Level 4) puerī — the boys puerōrum — of the boys puerīs — to (or for) the boys puerōs — the boys cum puerīs — with the boys
second declension -er (singular) as in **ager**	(Page 73) (Level 4) ager — the field agrī — of the field agrō — to (or for) the field agrum — the field in agrō — in the field
second declension -er (plural) as in **ager**	(Page 73) (Level 4) agrī — the fields agrōrum — of the fields agrīs — to (or for) the fields agrōs — the fields in agrīs — in the fields
Nouns that end with -**is** in the genitive singular belong to which declension?	(Page 75) (Level 4) the third declension
third declension (singular) as in **frāter**	(Page 75) (Level 4) frāter — the brother frātris — of the brother frātrī — to (or for) the brother frātrem — the brother cum frātre — with the brother
third declension (plural) as in **frāter**	(Page 75) (Level 4) frātrēs — the brothers frātrum — of the brothers frātribus — to (or for) the brothers frātrēs — the brothers cum frātribus — with the brothers

(front)	(back)
third declension (singular) as in **soror**	(Page 75) (Level 4) soror — the sister sorōris — of the sister sorōrī — to (or for) the sister sorōrem — the sister cum sorōre — with the sister
third declension (plural) as in **soror**	(Page 75) (Level 4) sorōrēs — the sisters sorōrum — of the sisters sorōribus — to (or for) the sisters sorōrēs — the sisters cum sorōribus — with the sisters
third declension i-stem (singular) as in **hostis**	(Page 79) (Level 4) hostis — the enemy hostis — of the enemy hostī — to (or for) the enemy hostem — the enemy cum hoste — with the enemy
third declension i-stem (plural) as in **hostis**	(Page 79) (Level 4) hostēs — the enemies hostium — of the enemies hostibus — to (or for) the enemies hostēs — the enemies cum hostibus — with the enemies
third declension i-stem (singular) as in **gēns**	(Page 80) (Level 4) gēns — the nation gentis — of the nation gentī — to (or for) the nation gentem — the nation cum gente — with the nation
third declension i-stem (plural) as in **gēns**	(Page 80) (Level 4) gentēs — the nations gentium — of the nations gentibus — to (or for) the nations gentēs — the nations cum gentibus — with the nations

(front)	(back)

third declension i-stem (singular) as in **urbs**	(Page 80) (Level 4) urbs — the city urbis — of the city urbī — to (or for) the city urbem — the city in urbe — in the city
third declension i-stem (plural) as in **urbs**	(Page 80) (Level 4) urbēs — the cities urbium — of the cities urbibus — to (or for) the cities urbēs — the cities in urbibus — in the cities
third declension i-stem neuter (singular)	(Page 81) (Level 4) mare — the sea maris — of the sea marī — to (or for) the sea mare — the sea in marī — in the sea
third declension i-stem neuter (plural)	(Page 81) (Level 4) maria — the seas marium — of the seas maribus — to (or for) the seas maria — the seas in maribus — in the seas
Verbs that end with -āre in the second principal part belong to which conjugation?	(Page 83) (Level 4) the first conjugation
How do you find the present stem of a **first** conjugation verb?	(Page 83) (Level 4) drop the -re from the second principal part

(front)	(back)
Verbs that end with -ēre in the second principal part belong to which conjugation?	(Page 83) (Level 4) the second conjugation
How do you find the present stem of a **second** conjugation verb?	(Page 83) (Level 4) drop the -re from the second principal part
second conjugation present active indicative	(Page 83) (Level 4) sedeō I sit sedēmus we sit sedēs you (sing.) sit sedētis you (pl.) sit sedet he (she, it) sits sedent they sit
Verbs that end with -ere in the second principal part belong to which conjugation?	(Page 87) (Level 4) the third conjugation
How do you find the present stem of a **third** conjugation verb?	(Page 87) (Level 4) drop the -ō from the first principal part
third conjugation present active indicative	(Page 87) (Level 4) dīcō I say dīcimus we say dīcis you (sing.) say dīcitis you (pl.) say dīcit he (she, it) says dīcunt they say

(front)	(back)
nōmen	(Page 91) (Level 4) nōminis (n.) name
faciō	(Page 91) (Level 4) facere fēcī factum I make, I do
veniō	(Page 91) (Level 4) venīre vēnī ventum I come
manus	(Page 93) (Level 4) manūs (f.) hand, band (of men)
audiō	(Page 93) (Level 4) audīre audīvī audītum I hear, I listen to
diēs	(Page 93) (Level 4) diēī (m. and f.) day

(front)	(back)
capiō	(Page 95) (Level 4) capere cēpī captum I take, I capture
sciō	(Page 95) (Level 4) scīre scīvī scītum I know
iter	(Page 95) (Level 4) itineris (n.) route, journey, march
inveniō	(Page 97) (Level 4) invenīre invēnī inventum I come upon, I find
fidēs	(Page 97) (Level 4) fideī (f.) faith, loyalty, pledge, confidence
pater	(Page 97) (Level 4) patris (m.) father (if plural: senators)

(front)	(back)
accipiō	(Page 99) (Level 4) accipere accēpī acceptum I receive, I accept
homō	(Page 99) (Level 4) hominis (m. or f.) human being, man
cōnsilium	(Page 99) (Level 4) cōnsilī (n.) plan, advice, foresight
reperiō	(Page 101) (Level 4) reperīre repperī repertum I find, I discover
spēs	(Page 101) (Level 4) speī (f.) hope
vēritās	(Page 101) (Level 4) vēritātis (f.) truth, trueness

(front)	(back)
senātus	(Page 103) (Level 4) senātus (m.) senate
multitūdō	(Page 103) (Level 4) multitūdinis (f.) great number, crowd
ecce	(Page 103) (Level 4) behold
third declension neuter (singular)	(Page 109) (Level 4) nōmen — the name nōminis — of the name nōminī — to (or for) the name nōmen — the name nōmine — with the name
third declension neuter (plural)	(Page 109) (Level 4) nōmina — the names nōminum — of the names nōminibus — to (or for) the names nōmina — the names nōminibus — with the names
How do you ask a question that expects a *yes* or *no* answer?	(Page 113) (Level 4) add -ne to the end of the first word in the sentence

(front)	(back)
How do you ask a question that expects a *yes* answer?	(Page 113) (Level 4) begin the sentence with the word nōnne
How do you ask a question that expects a *no* answer?	(Page 113) (Level 4) begin the sentence with the word num
Verbs that end with -ere in the second principal part **and** whose present stems end in -i- belong to which conjugation?	(Page 119) (Level 4) the third conjugation i-stem
How do you find the present stem of a **third** conjugation i-stem verb?	(Page 119) (Level 4) drop the -ō from the first principal part
third conjugation i-stem present active indicative	(Page 119) (Level 4) capiō — I take capimus — we take capis — you (sing.) take capitis — you (pl.) take capit — he (she, it) takes capiunt — they take
Nouns that end with -ūs in the genitive singular belong to which declension?	(Page 123) (Level 4) the fourth declension

(front)	(back)
fourth declension (singular)	(Page 123) (Level 4) manus the hand manūs of the hand manuī to (or for) the hand manum the hand in manū in the hand
fourth declension (plural)	(Page 123) (Level 4) manūs the hands manuum of the hands manibus to (or for) the hands manūs the hands in manibus in the hands
Verbs that end with -īre in the second principal part belong to which conjugation?	(Page 127) (Level 4) the fourth conjugation
How do you find the present stem of a **fourth** conjugation verb?	(Page 127) (Level 4) drop the -re from the second principal part
fourth conjugation present active indicative	(Page 127) (Level 4) audiō I hear audīmus we hear audīs you (sing.) hear audītis you (pl.) hear audit he (she, it) hears audiunt they hear
Nouns that end with -ēī or -eī in the genitive singular belong to which declension?	(Page 131) (Level 4) the fifth declension

(front)	(back)
fifth declension (singular) as in diēs	(Page 131) (Level 4) diēs — the day diēī — of the day diēī — to (or for) the day diem — the day diē — by means of the day
fifth declension (plural) as in diēs	(Page 131) (Level 4) diēs — the days diērum — of the days diēbus — to (or for) the days diēs — the days diēbus — by means of the days
fifth declension (singular) as in spēs	(Page 131) (Level 4) spēs — the hope speī — of the hope speī — to (or for) the hope spem — the hope spē — by means of the hope
fifth declension (plural) as in spēs	(Page 131) (Level 4) spēs — the hopes spērum — of the hopes spēbus — to (or for) the hopes spēs — the hopes spēbus — by means of the hopes
ergō	(Page 139) (Level 4) therefore, then
iūdicō	(Page 139) (Level 4) iūdicāre iūdicāvī iūdicātum I judge, I consider

(front)	(back)
oppidum	(Page 139) (Level 4) oppidī (n.) town
quōmodo	(Page 141) (Level 4) how?
lēx	(Page 141) (Level 4) lēgis (f.) law
dōnum	(Page 141) (Level 4) dōnī (n.) gift, present
magister	(Page 143) (Level 4) magistrī (m.) master, teacher, director
dux	(Page 143) (Level 4) ducis (m.) leader, guide

(front)	(back)
animal	(Page 143) (Level 4) animālis (n.) animal
habeō	(Page 145) (Level 4) habēre habuī habitum I have, I hold, I keep, I consider
pōnō	(Page 145) (Level 4) pōnere posuī positum I put, I set, I place, I locate
lapis	(Page 145) (Level 4) lapidis (m.) stone
adventus	(Page 147) (Level 4) adventūs (m.) arrival, approach
trādō	(Page 147) (Level 4) trādere trādidī trāditum I hand over, I surrender, I hand down

(front)	(back)
iaciō	(Page 147) (Level 4) iacere iēcī iactum I throw
portus	(Page 149) (Level 4) portūs (m.) harbor, port
potestās	(Page 149) (Level 4) potestātis (f.) power, opportunity
regō	(Page 149) (Level 4) regere rēxī rēctum I rule